A Guide to
Trance Land

A NORTON PROFESSIONAL BOOK

A Guide to Trance Land

A Practical Handbook of Ericksonian and Solution-Oriented Hypnosis

BILL O'HANLON

W. W. NORTON & COMPANY
New York • London

To Helen
my entrancing paramour

For information about permission to reproduce selections from this book, write to
Permissions, W. W. Norton & Company, Inc., 500 Fifth Avenue, New York, NY 10110

For information about special discounts for bulk purchases, please contact W. W. Norton
Special Sales at specialsales@wwnorton.com or 800-233-4830

Manufacturing by R. R. Donnelley Bloomsburg
Book design by Gilda Hannah
Production manager: Leeann Graham

Library of Congress Cataloging-in-Publication Data

O'Hanlon, William Hudson.
   A guide to trance land : a practical handbook of Ericksonian and
solution-oriented hypnosis / Bill O'Hanlon. — 1st ed.
       p. cm.
   Includes bibliographical references and index.
   ISBN 978-0-393-70578-2 (pbk.)
   1. Hypnotism—Therapeutic use. I. Title.
   RC495.O337 2009
   616.89'162—dc22

                                                2008055982

ISBN: 978-0-393-70578-2 (pbk.)

W. W. Norton & Company, Inc., 500 Fifth Avenue, New York, N.Y. 10110
        www.wwnorton.com
W. W. Norton & Company Ltd., Castle House, 75/76 Wells Street, London W1T 3QT

1 2 3 4 5 6 7 8 9 0

Contents

Acknowledgments

Thank you to Milton Erickson, for taking me on as his student and gardener; to Stephen Gilligan, for his friendship, regular hospitality, and trance logic; and to my editors at W. W. Norton —Deborah Malmud for her support and encouragement, and Kristen Holt-Browning for her attention to detail and sunny attitude, which put me in a nice, relaxing editing trance.

Preface

Welcome to trance land! I have spent a lot of time in this territory over the past 30 years (I know that carbon dates me, but I promise I don't feel that old), both personally and as a guide for others. I have written a couple of other books on trance and its use in change work (*Solution-Oriented Hypnosis* and *Taproots*, both also published by W. W. Norton) and I decided it was time to revisit the subject.

Many well-known psychotherapists (Freud, Fritz Perls, developer of Gestalt therapy; Jay Haley, creator of strategic therapy; Stephen Gilligan, originator of the self-relations approach; behavioral psychiatrist Joseph Wolpe, developer of systematic desensitization; not to mention one of my main influences, Milton Erickson) used hypnosis early in their careers, before they went on to develop their unique approaches to change. I don't think this was a coincidence. Hypnosis can teach us many things about how the human mind, perceptions, and emotions function. It can also show how to help people shift those perceptions, mental processes, and emotions to resolve problems. Recent discoveries in neuroscience have pointed up the amazing plasticity of the brain and the mutability of habits (see Norman Doidge's *The Brain That Changes Itself* as a prime example). Hypnotherapists have known about this plasticity for some time. Just watch a stage hypnotist convince a hypnotized person that the tart lemon he is biting into is actually a sweet orange.

Many of the practitioners cited above moved on from hypnosis after their early years. Some of us, however, stick with hypnosis, as I have over many years. I still haven't come to the end of what I think I can learn from trance. Hypnosis, for me, is an endlessly fascinating subject. At the same time, it has become clearer and simpler to me. This book is a result of many years of teaching professionals how to compellingly invite their clients into trance and to help those clients reduce or eliminate the suffering that brought them to seek help.

This book is the third in a line of guidebooks that began with a book I coauthored with Sandy Beadle *(A Guide to Possibility Land)*, who did much to shape the form of the text, including the images that are scattered throughout the pages. Her research in the area of instructional design showed that breaking the points up into small chunks and using images made them more memorable and effective. Whether those were the elements that made a difference or not, that first guidebook and the subsequent one *(A Guide to Inclusive Therapy)* proved to be sufficiently popular and brought such nice comments that I began hatching a plan to write at least one more.

Hypnosis can be intimidating to people, so I have tried to make it friendly, nonintimidating, and non-frightening. I hope I have succeeded, and I hope you enjoy this book deeply (and more deeply).

BILL O'HANLON
Santa Fe, New Mexico,
September 2008

Introduction to Solution-Oriented or Ericksonian Hypnosis

There are two major types of hypnosis: authoritarian and permissive. The tradition I practice within, which I have come to call solution-oriented hypnosis, is permissive. I studied with the late psychiatrist Milton H. Erickson a few years before his death in 1980 (I was actually Erickson's gardener while I was in graduate school studying to be a marriage and family therapist, since I couldn't afford to pay him for his teaching).

There are both philosophical and technical differences between authoritarian hypnosis and the permissive approach. To illustrate the Ericksonian tradition, let's start with a story or two.

The first was one Dr. Erickson used to tell students quite regularly. When he was a child, growing up in rural Wisconsin in the early 1900s, he and some friends came across a horse that had obviously thrown its rider. None of them recognized the horse or knew to whom it belonged. After catching the horse and calming it down, young Erickson declared that he would take the horse back to its owner. "How are you going to do that?" asked his friends. "You don't even know whose horse this is."

But Erickson just got on the horse and spurred it on. Some miles down the road, the horse veered into a farm. When

Erickson and the horse arrived before the waiting farmer, he thanked Erickson for bringing the horse home, but asked how he knew to bring the horse there, since they didn't know one another. Erickson replied, "I didn't know where the horse should go, but he did. I just kept him on the road and moving."

That is a cornerstone of the permissive approach to hypnosis: the person knows the way. The hypnotherapist's task is to keep the client moving.

The second story is one told by a child psychiatrist who was a student of Erickson's. Erickson was teaching a workshop in San Francisco and the child psychiatrist brought one of his oppositional-defiant teenage patients, Ed, to work with Erickson, since he wasn't making much progress with the boy in treatment. He expected Erickson to hypnotize the boy, but when the boy came up and sat before Erickson and the group of workshop participants, Erickson mentioned that the psychiatrist had told him about Ed getting into trouble. Erickson then looked at Ed and said simply, "I really don't know how you are going to change your behavior." Then he thanked Ed for coming, and the boy and his psychiatrist left the workshop. The psychiatrist was mystified by this turn of events and decided that perhaps Erickson had decided not to work with Ed. But over the

next few months the boy showed a remarkable improvement in his situation. When the psychiatrist thought back to that brief encounter, he realized that Erickson had actually made an intervention that day. He had implied that Ed would change his behavior and then left the boy to his own devices as to how he would change it.

These two stories illustrate the main differences between the two hypnotic traditions, both in how they approach trance induction and how they approach treatment.

Traditional hypnotherapy relies on the authority and power of the hypnotist to "get" the person into trance. It also taps into suggestibility, which is required for success in this more authoritarian approach. Once the client is in trance, the hypnotherapist has a clear direction for trance (uncovering repressed or forgotten trauma that may be creating present problems; implanting new, more positive beliefs; and so on). I see this as an outside-in approach. The hypnotist is trying to get new stuff to happen from the outside and is the expert on what is going on with the person he or she is treating and what that person needs to do to get better.

The solution-oriented approach, in contrast, is based more on evocation than suggestion. Echoing the title of a book on Erickson's work (*The Answer Within* by Steve and Carol Lankton), solution-oriented hypnotherapists hold that people have answers and knowledge within themselves that can be tapped and released with the right invitations. The right invitations are the ones that really resonate with a particular person. That's why this approach, while it has a set of generalized guidelines, does not have any formulas. Every trance induction is different. Every treatment is different. Some people will discover some repressed memories. Others will merely shift their thinking. Still others will perceive strange sensations or colors that will become meaningful and lead them to change. The person is the expert; the hypnotherapist is merely the facilitator of the evoked answers or responses.

Differences Between Solution-Oriented and Traditional Hypnosis

Permissive versus Authoritarian
Evocation versus Suggestion
Expert versus Collaboration and Nonexpert Stance

May I Suggest Being Less Suggestive? Contrasting Authoritarian and Permissive Hypnosis

In authoritarian hypnosis, the hypnotherapist must establish his or her authority to cause things to happen with patients or subjects. The phrasing used in this approach typically involves words like *will*, *are*, *won't*, or *can't*.

Here are some sample phrases:

You are going deeply into trance.

You will not be able to open your eyes.

Your hand will lift all the way up to your face without you
being able to stop it.

You can't feel your jaw or mouth. It is numb.

Your eyes are getting heavier and heavier.

When I snap my fingers, you will come all the way out of
trance.

The hypnotist becomes the authority on the people's experience (Virginia Satir called this "mind reading"), telling them
what they are feeling or what they will feel. Or the hypnotherapist becomes the author of the experience: He or she tells subjects or patients that they will do something and it happens just
as the hypnotherapist said it would.

In the permissive tradition, the hypnotherapist uses words
like *may, can, could, might*, or *don't have to*, and provides multiple
options for response.

Some sample phrases in this mode might be:

You can go as deeply into trance as is comfortable for you
right now.

Your eyes might be feeling heavy. They might stay open and
you might just decide to close them on your own.

You may go anywhere you want. You don't even have to
listen to what I am saying.

You might not even notice that you are going into trance.

There is no right way or wrong way to respond. You can
find your own way of going into trance.

In addition to these technical and phrasing differences, there
is a philosophical difference in these two traditions. The author-

itarian approach views the hypnotherapist as the expert who knows both what is wrong with the person seeking help and the appropriate path to correct the problem. The hypnotherapist in this tradition might discover or decide that the person has an early trauma that has created the current difficulty. The appropriate intervention might then be to age regress the person back to that original traumatic experience and rework it. Or it might be to instill new, more helpful beliefs about the

individual or the situation. Whatever the intervention or the analysis, it typically comes from the hypnotherapist.

In contrast, in the permissive approach, the hypnotherapist studiously avoids being the expert on the problem or the solution. He or she merely provides a context in which people can come to their own conclusions and use whatever resources emerge to solve the problem.

In other words, the permissive approach is evocative rather than suggestive. This difference is grounded in a sense that people have resources and wisdom within and in their social contexts.

An authoritarian hypnotherapist might say:

Go all the way back to a time before you were 5 years old and find a moment that changed everything. Go deeper and deeper into trance and go all the way back.

You will be more and more confident in social situations.

The person is being directed to do or think or feel something. The hypnotherapist has an idea of what will help and suggests a solution or path to solution. It is an outside-in approach.

The permissive approach is evocative, an inside-out orientation.

Some examples of what a permissive, evocative approach might involve when the person is in trance follow:

> I really don't know how you will resolve this issue, but I do know that something inside you knows what needs to happen and to whom you might need to talk to move forward.
>
> You only need to go as deeply as is appropriate to connect with the resources you need to feel better and get clear on what is next for you.

Suggestion Versus Evocation

These language distinctions reflect the shift from the old notion of hypnosis as being primarily about suggestion and reprogramming to it being about evocation. In this approach to hypnosis, the hypnotherapist is not trying to correct some faulty beliefs or traumatically installed thinking by replacing those beliefs or thoughts with new, more healthy ones. (I find myself wondering: "healthy" according to whom?) Instead, he or she is working to evoke abilities and resources that could resolve the presenting issue.

This is not a trivial difference or mere technical shift: the goals are different.

Suggestion

Authority/mind reading/prediction
Use the word *are*
Use the words *will* or *won't*
Use the word *can't*

Evocation

Permission/inviting/opening possibilities
Use the word *can*
Use the words *might, may,* or *could*
Give multiple-choice options

With this introduction to orient you, let's get down to brass tacks and specifics. Next, we will break out and detail the minimal elements and skills needed to invite a person into trance. In keeping with the form of the previous books, each skill or section will have its own page or two, making the book readable in bite-sized chunks. You can read the book straight through or dip into it in tiny pieces, whatever suits your time and inclination.

Ready? Put your seat backs all the way into the upright position and your tray tables into the locked position. Here we go, heading for trance land.

A Guide to
Trance Land

Elements of Solution-Oriented Induction

Here, we'll take up the minimal elements that can serve to invite a person powerfully and compellingly into trance using this approach.

I have divided these methods into elements (and sometimes subelements within the main method) to make them easy to learn. Obviously in hypnotherapeutic practice, many of these are used together or simultaneously. But for learning purposes, making them discrete elements makes them easier to distinguish and master.

1. Permission

Your task in using the skills offered in this first section is to create an atmosphere of acceptance, comfort, nonintrusion, and validation in which the person cannot fail or do anything wrong. This safe and nonpressurized atmosphere goes a long way toward dissolving any resistance or barriers most people have about going into trance. If you do this part well, the rest of the induction and treatment will typically go more smoothly and easily.

Erickson had this notion he called *utilization*. He considered it to be one of his two original contributions to the field of hypnosis (the other being the interspersal technique, which we'll cover in a later section). The essence of utilization is that the hypnotherapist should accept and use whatever the person presents as part and parcel of the trance and the treatment. If people pace back and forth in the office, the hypnotherapist does not insist that they sit down, uncross their arms and legs, or relax and close their eyes before beginning the trance. No, the pacing will be accepted and used as the way a person will start the trance.

I was hypnotizing a 10-year-old boy and he began to giggle during the trance induction. I said, "What a nice way to go into trance; to giggle your way in." This resulted in him giggling even harder. I responded, "Most adults are so serious about trance, but I think giggling might be a fun way to go deeper." I kept on in this vein for a time, adding the other elements that you will read about in this book, and gradually he stopped giggling. When he began to emerge from the trance about 30 minutes later, however, he giggled his way out of trance. This young man had the giggle method of going into and coming out of trance.

Another person I worked with kept up a running commentary on what was happening within her as she went into trance: "Oh, my eyes are getting heavy; I am starting to see colors in my mind, purples and green; my hands are getting numb; this is interesting." Now, most people don't speak much as they are going into trance, but there is no law against it. She had the commentary method of going into trance.

Yet another person wiggled around in his chair while going into trance. Most people become more still, but he had the wiggle method of going into trance. I accepted and validated this behavior as a legitimate way of going into trance.

The point: each person has his or her own method of going into trance. In this approach, none of it is seen as resistance, only the person's unique response and experience. Any response (short of people doing violence to themselves or others) is seen as acceptable and even encouraged and included as part of the hypnotic process rather than a block to it.

There are several variations on this method, which are detailed in the sections that follow.

1.1 Accept, Normalize, Reassure and Validate Whatever the Person Presents

To create an atmosphere in which it is easy for people to go into trance, actively accept whatever experience they are having. Give them the sense that whatever they are doing is okay and part of the process of going into trance. This includes any concerns, fears, resistance, or distractions they may have.

When people first encounter hypnosis, they often have either fixed ideas of what hypnosis is ("I'll be knocked out and won't hear or know a thing") or they have fears ("Someone will control me and make me do things I wouldn't want to do in my everyday life"). So I often spend a little time eliciting those ideas or concerns and reassuring them that those things are not what hypnosis is about. Or I reassure them that those concerns are normal and common.

When they are going into trance, while they are in trance, or after trance, I sometimes do the same thing: I reassure them that their trance experiences are part of the spectrum of things that people typically experience with hypnosis.

Client: I am not sure I believe in hypnosis. I am very rational.

Hypnotherapist: You don't need to believe in it for it to work. It's fine to be skeptical.

Client: I am afraid of losing control.

Hypnotherapist: That's a common concern for people about to go into trance. In this kind of hypnosis, it's not about me controlling you or you being out of control.

Client: My eyelids keep fluttering. Is that normal?

Hypnotherapist: I've seen it many times. It's one of the things that can happen in trance.

1.2 Give Permission To

There are typically two varieties of permission we use in induction: *permission to* and *permission not to have to*. *Permission to* is accomplished by using words and phrases such as *You can*, *It's okay to*, *You might*, *You are okay if you*, *You could*, and so on. Either imagine or elicit from your clients what they are experiencing that might be a distraction, a barrier, or a concern for them and give them permission to have that experience or concern. This typically dissolves that concern or makes it less of a barrier to the induction.

Hypnotherapist: You may be distracted by the sounds around you. That's okay.

Hypnotherapist: You may not think that you can go into a trance or that you will go into a trance today and that is fine.

Hypnotherapist: Wherever you go, that's okay. There's no right way or wrong way to go into trance. Everyone has his or her own pathway in.

Hypnotherapist: You can make whatever adjustments you need to make: physical, emotional, psychological, or any other adjustments.

Hypnotherapist: You can change any words I say that aren't right for you into other words that are right for you or just tune them out.

1.3 Give Permission Not to Have To

This is the opposite side of the coin from the first kind of permission. Here we give people permission not to have to experience certain things that they are feeling pressured to experience. This involves the use of words and phrases like *You don't have to*, *It's okay not to*, and so on.

Hypnotherapist: You don't have to focus on anything in particular.

Hypnotherapist: You don't have to relax to go into trance.

Hypnotherapist: You don't even have to listen to my voice.

Hypnotherapist: You don't have to believe you are going into trance. You can just follow your experience.

1.4 Note and Include Any Distractions, Difficulties, Negativity, or Resistance

The task here is to take off the pressure the person might be putting on himself or herself to "do it right." In this approach, any difficulties, fears, concerns, and resistance can be an integral part of the process. The way to make these things integral is to note them, acknowledge them to the person, and include them.

Hypnotherapist: You can notice the sounds around you. You may be consciously distracted by them or you may tune them out.

Hypnotherapist: You might be analyzing every word that I am saying. That's okay.

Hypnotherapist: Some people have the idea that they will be knocked out and unaware of anything while in trance. You can be thinking at the same time as you are going into trance.

You can be divided in some way; part of you going into trance and part of you observing the process.

Hypnotherapist: You say you're getting frightened. It's okay to be scared and keep going into trance, if that's okay with you.

Hypnotherapist: You don't have to make anything happen. It's more like you're allowing things to happen, but if you're having trouble allowing, that's okay too.

1.5 Use Possibility Words and Phrases (Rather Than Mind-Reading or Prediction Language)

These are words that open up possibilities and invite people to have experiences rather than telling them what to feel, experience, or do or what they will feel, experience, or do. These words and phrases include *might, could, can, perhaps, might not,* and so on. Be careful not to use phrases and words like *are, will, must, should,* and other words and phrases that imply that you, the hypnotist, have special knowledge about what the person is feeling, experiencing, or thinking or will experience, do, think, or feel.

Hypnotherapist: You can go as deeply into trance as is comfortable for you right now.

Hypnotherapist: Your eyes might be feeling heavy, or they might stay open and you might just decide to close them on your own.

Hypnotherapist: You may go anywhere you want. You don't even have to listen to what I am saying.

Hypnotherapist: You might not even notice that you are going into trance.

Hypnotherapist: There is no right way or wrong way to respond. You can find your own way of going into trance.

1.6 Give Multiple Possibilities for Responding

If you give many possibilities for response, people are likely to find one or more that will happen or work for them. This can also help people feel a sense of control.

Hypnotherapist: One of your hands might start to lift, or you might just notice a slight shift in the sensations of the hand, or it might start to feel as if it's glued to your thigh.

Hypnotherapist: You could attend to everything I am saying or you could drift off into your own thoughts.

Creating Connection and Opening Possibilities
For trance, trance phenomena, and experiential shifts

This, then, is the first skill you need to master to do skillful hypnosis in this style. You need to be able to help people feel comfortable and not pressured. You also need to be able to make a solid connection with them, which the methods in this first section can help you do.

Validation involves giving the verbal and nonverbal message that the person's experience and style of responding are valid and within the range of normal or legitimate experience and response.

Possibilities language is all about not boxing yourself or your clients in during the induction. There should be no way for them or you to fail during induction. Every response is included and there is no pressure to "do it right." Giving multiple options for legitimate response is a good way to use possibilities language.

Hypnotherapist: Your mind might drift away. Your mind might be analyzing what I am saying, or you might shift between the two ways of attending, or you might be doing something else altogether that I can't even know. And that's all okay.

Connecting is all about keeping connected to people while you are doing trance by avoiding saying or doing anything that is invalidating or jarring and might sever the connection. It also involves closely observing people so you are in tune with where they are and how they are responding.

Master:

Observation
Permission
Validation
Possibilities language
Responsiveness to the person's responses
Connecting

Avoid:

Jarring statements and actions
Unhelpful mind reading
Pushing people

2. Presuppositon

The coauthor of the first book I wrote, *Shifting Contexts*, was Jim Wilk. Jim was a very future-oriented person, sometimes too much so (he was always thinking that his ship would come in and pay off his substantial debts). Once, we were talking on the phone and he mentioned that someone had hired him to give a workshop on Ericksonian hypnosis. "What are you going to do?" I asked, since I knew he had only read about but never actually practiced hypnosis. "I'll practice in the months before I have to give the presentation," he replied confidently.

Well, time rolled on. Jim's workplace wouldn't give him permission to use hypnosis in his work and he never did get a chance to practice. After he presented the workshop, I asked him how it went. "Fantastic!"

"Did you do any demonstrations?"

"Oh, yes. They went well."

"My God, Jim, you are incredible. How did you pull it off?"

"Well, when it came time to do the demonstrations, I was terrified. But I came up with an idea. I would just imagine that Milton Erickson was standing right behind me actually doing the hypnosis and all I had to do was report what was happening and speculate on what was likely to happen."

So he would say things like, "I see that your eyelids are fluttering. I wonder whether you know you are going into a trance." Or, "How deeply will you go into a trance? Neither one of us knows, but we will find out." Or, "Which hand will lift up first? We'll have to wait to discover which one your unconscious chooses."

That way, Jim took the pressure off himself. But what he was actually doing was a lot of presupposing without telling the person to do anything. He assumed that Erickson would get the person into trance and help him or her develop hand levitation.

This is a good strategy to use as a hypnotherapist. You don't actually have to make anyone do anything. You can make indirect invitations.

Erickson himself had a very striking example of using presupposition to induce trance.

One time when he was giving a workshop, Dr. Erickson announced that he wanted to give a demonstration of hypnosis. He called for a volunteer from the participants in the workshop and when one came up on stage and seated himself, Erickson merely looked at him without saying a word. The person 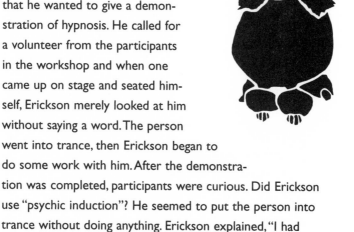 went into trance, then Erickson began to do some work with him. After the demonstration was completed, participants were curious. Did Erickson use "psychic induction"? He seemed to put the person into trance without doing anything. Erickson explained, "I had defined the situation as one in which trance would be demonstrated. He came up and when I didn't do anything, he went into trance. It was implied that he would go into trance."

So your task using this set of skills is to presume that the person will go into trance and have various hypnotic experiences. (Later I will suggest using the same method to bring about the therapeutic changes you and the client are aiming for.)

2.1 Before

One of the easiest presuppositions to use is the "before" form of presupposition. This is where you assume that the person is going to go into trance sometime in the future.

Read these two questions:

Have you ever been in trance?
Have you ever been in trance before?

The person you ask either of these questions may answer the same way, but the implication in the second question is different. The second question implies that sometime in the future (the near future if they have come to you for trance work), the person will be going into a trance.

Hypnotherapist: Before you go into trance, I want to talk with you about some common myths about hypnosis.

Hypnotherapist: Don't go into trance yet. Let's get clear on what you'd like to accomplish when you're in trance.

2.2 After

This form of presupposition is the opposite of the "before" form. Here you are presuming that the person will go into a trance by mentioning or asking about things that will or could occur after the trance is over.

Hypnotherapist: After you come out of a trance, you may remember everything that happened or it may be like a dream that fades more and more as time goes on.
You can also use verb tense in a deliberate way to imply the end of trance.

Hypnotherapist: How was that? Was the trance different from what you expected?

2.3 Rate

In this third form of presupposition, you never doubt that the person will go into trance, but only speculate or ask about the rate at which he or she will go into trance.

Hypnotherapist: How quickly do you think you can go into trance? I don't know. It's different for each person.

Hypnotherapist: You can go into trance at your own rate and pace. You don't have to go any more quickly than is appropriate for you.

2.4 Timing

Initially, timing may seem the same as rate, but this form of presupposition speculates or asks about the exact timing of the trance, while still presuming that trance will happen.

Hypnotherapist: When will you go all the way into trance? I really don't know and you really don't know. Your unconscious will decide and let both of us know.

Hypnotherapist: Will you go into a trance now or not until the next session? Time will tell.

2.5 Depth

In this form of presupposition, you are speculating or asking about how deeply the person will go into trance. Remember, you are not questioning or casting doubt on whether the person will enter trance, only the depth of the trance.

Hypnotherapist: Will you go into a light, medium, or deep trance?

Hypnotherapist: You only need to go as deeply as you need to go to get the results you want.

Hypnotherapist: How much more deeply will you go?

2.6 Means, Pathways, or Method

Here you're using speculation about how the person will go into trance as a medium for presuming that he or she will go into trance.

Hypnotherapist: Will you find yourself losing track of your body as you go into trance? I don't know. Perhaps you will just start drifting into your own thoughts or experiences as you go deeper.

Hypnotherapist: There are a number of different ways to go into trance. I'm sure yours will be as unique as your fingerprints.

2.7 Awareness

In this form of presupposition, you are speculating or questioning only whether the person has noticed, is noticing, or will notice something about going into trance, not that the person will go into trance.

Hypnotherapist: I wonder what you are aware of as you go deeper into trance.

Hypnotherapist: Perhaps you are noticing some different sensations. Perhaps you're very focused on my voice as you're going deeper.

Hypnotherapist: Have you noticed the shifts in your breathing as you continue to go into trance?

Hypnotherapist: Are you aware of going deeper yet? It is okay if you aren't.

2.8 Verb Tenses

Although I have discussed verb tenses in earlier parts of this section, let's visit this skill in more detail. Erickson used verb tenses in various ways—to imply change and trance, to shift time orientation, and to confuse. ("And you will then have known what I will have been expecting you to have learned," I once heard him say.)

To keep things simple, we'll stick to the past, present, and future.

For example, if you would like to invite the person to more fully experience something that is in the past or the future, you could switch to the present tense.

Hypnotherapist: Where are you now? What are you seeing?

Hypnotherapist: Okay, it's now 5 years in the future and you have gotten through that trouble you had so many years ago and come out the other side long ago. What are you doing in your life right now?

As we discussed earlier, if you wanted to imply that trance was over without formally telling the person to come out of trance, you could use the past tense:

Hypnotherapist: How was that? Was that different from what you expected?

Obviously there are many variations on the use of verb tense and some of you may want to explore this skill more, but we will leave it there for now.

3. Splitting

The human mind has a tendency to split things apart, to make distinctions. In Western cultures we divide our calendars into B.C. and A.D. We divide the day up into hours and minutes; the year into days and months and seasons. We can use this tendency to facilitate the process of trance induction and treatment. This is called *splitting*. By splitting I mean two things: dividing previously unified concepts or experiences into parts or creating new distinctions.

3.1 Make Distinctions

In hypnosis, the distinctions we propose are often between the conscious and the unconscious, but they could be between any aspect of experience and another aspect of experience. We could propose, as did Descartes, a split between the mind and the body. Or between the front of the mind and the back of the mind. Or one part of the person and another part.

Hypnotherapist: You have a conscious mind and an unconscious mind.

Hypnotherapist: You could listen with your mind, but I am really talking to your body.

Hypnotherapist: One part of you could be confused and another part of you can understand perfectly.

3.2 Split Something Previously Considered One Thing into Two or More Parts

Here the hypnotherapist reconsiders something previously thought of as one thing, instead breaking it down into at least two parts. This is sometimes done to bypass resistance and sometimes to shift thinking.

Hypnotherapist: You could have the feeling that you have had when watching a favorite scene in a movie without remembering what that scene is.

Client: I'm afraid of hypnosis because I like to be in control.

Hypnotherapist: Well, there is old-style hypnosis, which involved the hypnotist controlling the subject. What I do is the new hypnosis. You'll be in control. What I'll be is more like a coach, suggesting possibilities for things you can do inside. These possibilities are only invitations, you will decide which to take up or respond to.

Note that here the hypnotherapist has proposed a split between old-style hypnosis and new hypnosis.

3.3 Make the Split Nonverbally as Well as Verbally

It's possible and important to make splits nonverbally as well as verbally. Nonverbal splitting is usually done using different voice tones, voice volumes, and spatial locations for the voice. If the person's eyes are open, there could be visual splitting.

Erickson often used different voice tones and volumes when he was speaking about the unconscious than when he was speaking about conscious processes. He also often leaned to one side when speaking of the unconscious and to the other when speaking of the conscious. That way, even when the person's eyes were closed, he or she could hear these changes (often not consciously noticing them) and respond appropriately to the distinction.

4. Linking

The element complementary to splitting is *linking*, which involves joining together two previously unrelated or unlinked concepts or experiences. You could also think of this as creating associations. Again, this seems to be a natural human tendency. You eat a certain food and become ill, and after that unpleasant experience, that food tends to bring up unpleasant gastro-intestinal sensations (sorry about the pun). In this hypnotic skill, the hypnotherapist is deliberately proposing associations for hypnotic and therapeutic purposes.

4.1 Join Things Together Verbally

There are many forms of verbal linking and I have provided a list of some of them here so you can get an idea of the range. Of course, you can create your own new forms of linking once you understand the concept, and I encourage you to be creative.

Typical verbal forms of linking:
While you ____, you can ____.
As you ____, you can ____.

When ____ happens, you can ____.

You may not be able to ____ until ____.

As you begin to ____, you can notice ____.

As ____ happens, ____ can begin to happen more and more.

The more your conscious mind ____, the easier it can be for your unconscious mind to ____.

After ____ happens, ____ can continue/happen/begin.

The more ____, the more ____.

The more ____, the less ____.

Hypnotherapist: As you are listening to the sound of my voice, you can go deeper into trance.

Hypnotherapist: The more distracted you are by the sounds outside, the easier it can be for your unconscious mind to get free from the dominance of your conscious mind and go do its work.

Hypnotherapist: When that hand touches your face, you can go even deeper into trance.

Hypnotherapist: As you begin to go into trance, your unconscious can begin to prepare to make the changes you need to make to feel better, to be more comfortable, to get some relief.

4.2 Link Something in Your Behavior or Speaking to Something the Person is Doing

You could link certain voice tones or rates of speech, or non-verbal actions, to something in the person's behavior or speaking. As you gradually change your behavior or speaking, the person is likely to follow, since your behavior and theirs are now linked.

Like splitting, linking is often done nonverbally. As an example, Erickson once did this with a man who paced back and forth in his office and spoke in an anxious, hurried way. He told Erickson he was so anxious that he couldn't sit down and talk about his problem; he was on the verge of running out of the office, and pacing and talking compulsively was all that was keeping him there. Erickson began speaking very quickly to the man, matching his rate of speech and walking. Erickson then almost imperceptibly slowed his rate of speech and the man began slowing his own walking and speaking. The two had become linked.

Hypnotherapist: You could find your hand lifting [timing this word to the person's hand lifting slightly with his or her inhalation] automatically.

Hypnotherapist: [leaning to the right] Consciously, you might wonder whether you can go into trance; [leaning to the left] and your unconscious mind is already preparing to go deeper.

Next we'll take up a combination of splitting and linking that Erickson called *interspersal*.

A CRYPTIC COMMUNICATION
Learning Interspersal

When I studied with Milton Erickson, he was fond of presenting me with riddles, which I never solved.

One day, he wrote out a phrase on a piece of paper. Because he had some muscular weakness due to his polio and its aftereffects, his handwriting was a bit uneven.

He told me that the phrase he had written was a reproduction of a note that was given to a staff member of a psychiatric hospital in which he had worked by a patient who had never spoken a word during his hospitalization. The staff all looked at the note and couldn't decipher any useful meaning in it. But Erickson could. He asked me what the patient was trying to communicate. I couldn't work it out.

Here is the note:

I AM GOING to a place where there are no
bad, MAD people.

5. Interspersal

Erickson thought he had made two original and unique contributions to the practice of hypnosis. Interspersal was one of
them (the other was utilization). Interspersal is a combination
of splitting and linking. Some parts of the communication from
the hypnotist to the person are nonverbally emphasized (and
are thus linked to one another) and therefore are split off from
the rest of the message.

Erickson maintained that people communicate like this quite
regularly, so the hypnotherapist is just using a form of complex
communication that everyone understands at an unconsciously
processed level. He said sometimes his patients would be talking about some subject and would emphasize a word or phrase,
thereby alerting Erickson to one of their concerns. For example, the person would be talking about a problem at work and
say: "I've just got to divorce myself from my boss's criticism. I
can't let him tear me down." Erickson would eventually inquire
about the person's marriage.

In the example in the box at left (A Cryptic Communication), the answer to the riddle was that the patient was trying
to say, without saying, that he was going mad. It turned out that
he was terrified. If he spoke his fears aloud, he was certain they

would become real. Therefore he had to disguise the message, because he was desperate to get help but couldn't say what he was worried about.

So, interspersal is nonverbally emphasizing or distinguishing certain words or phrases to create a message within a message. This can be accomplished using several nonverbal channels.

5.1 Emphasizing Through Voice Volume

The first channel involves slightly lowering or raising your voice volume on the words or phrases you want to intersperse. It doesn't particularly matter if you raise or lower your voice volume. The main thing is to link a consistent shift to certain phrases.

In the examples below, the bold words or phrases are the interspersed ones.

Hypnotherapist: I don't know how quickly you [this next phrase said slightly louder than the previous words] **can go into trance**.

Hypnotherapist: You don't really have to [this next phrase said slightly softer than the previous words] **go deeper**.

Hypnotherapist: You may be convinced that you can't change or that you may not be able to **change very much**.

5.2 Emphasizing Through Voice Location

In this variation, the hypnotherapist changes voice location for certain phrases.

> **Hypnotherapist:** I don't know how quickly you [this next phrase said while leaning to the left] **can make those changes you really want to make.**

> **Hypnotherapist:** You don't really have to [this next phrase said while moving forward] **change.**

5.2 Inadvertent Interspersal

Warning: Be careful not to emphasize phrases you don't want to or that might not be helpful to people.

I like to joke that we parents are sometimes very poor hypnotists. "Don't **spill that milk**," we yell across the room and there goes the milk. In a similar way, we can give inadvertent suggestions to our clients and patients, within the context of hypnosis or outside it.

> **Hypnotherapist:** I know you are in a **great deal of pain.**

> **Hypnotherapist:** You are really **stuck.**

> **Hypnotherapist:** You are **sick and tired** of being sick and tired.

There is an easy way around this. Just train yourself to emphasize the last word or phrase in the sentence. Then take care not to use negative words or phrases in that place in the sentence. (This idea might help your parenting as well.)

6. Introduction to the Other Elements

In this chapter, I will discuss some other helpful elements in creating a trance. Because each of them only merits a short discussion, I have put them all in one chapter rather than devoting a whole chapter to each, as I did with the previous elements. We'll cover Description, Truisms, Matching, Guiding Attention and Associations, and the Confusion Technique.

6.1 Description

When doing hypnosis, it is important to maintain both connection and credibility with subjects. One way to do this is to describe only what you can verify with your senses that the person is showing you. That means you must be careful not to assume or guess about internal states and processes, because if you are wrong or off in your guesses or interpretations, it might be jarring to the person and disrupt his or her experience and your connection with him or her.

Erickson did a dramatic demonstration one time to illustrate the importance of observing and not going beyond the evidence of your senses. He arranged for a person to enter a lecture hall, walking in only a few steps. He had arranged the students on both sides of the room and then asked them to write down a description of the person. After a short time, the person walked the several steps backward out of the lecture hall, never turning around.

When some of the students began to read their written description of the person, the point of the exercise quickly became clear. Students on the right side of the room described a person who had blue eyes, and students on the left side of the room described a person who had green eyes. It turned out the person had two different colored eyes. Erickson emphasized to the students that he was training them to observe and not go beyond what they could directly observe. The lesson stuck.

This skill, then, has two components: observation and description. But what you will say to the subject involves description. To do this well, you must observe carefully and well. That is why I usually recommend sitting directly in front of the person, with a full view of the front of his or her body. Description is telling people what you can observe about their behavior on an ongoing basis, especially mentioning those things that are changing. This has the effect of garnering credibility for you, as well as directing their attention to those aspects of their experience.

Hypnotherapist: Your eyelids are fluttering.

Hypnotherapist: Your feet are in your shoes on the floor. You're sitting in the chair, arms on the arms of the chair at the moment, and blinking.

Hypnotherapist: Your fingers are moving, ever so slightly, in a jerky fashion.

6.2 Truisms

Truisms are statements that are obviously true and don't require observation or guessing about what the person is experiencing. Trusims go beyond observation, but are typically not jarring (as guessing incorrectly about a person's experience might be). Truisms might also be statements that sound generally true but that are hard to check.

Hypnotherapist: There is a lot going on inside you.

Hypnotherapist: While I've been talking to you, various changes have occurred.

Hypnotherapist: Your unconscious is active on your behalf throughout the day and the night while you are sleeping.

Hypnotherapist: Many things can change when you are in trance.

6.3 Matching

Matching involves the hypnotherapist aligning some parts of his or her behavior or communication with something similar in the client's behavior. Another aspect of matching is to carefully attend to things that are changing and match those changes.

6.3.1 Matching rhythm

Typically, the hypnotist in this approach matches the rhythm of his speaking with the rhythm of the person's breathing, but there are other ways to match rhythms as well. You might notice that a person is moving her foot up and down in a regular way and then match your speaking rhythm to that rhythm as you begin to do trance, or throughout the whole hypnotic session.

6.3.2 Matching Body Behavior

The hypnotist sometimes mirrors the person's posture or movements as a way of joining and connecting. For example, when a person crosses and uncrosses his legs, the hypnotist also crosses and uncrosses her legs. Another way to match body behavior is to vary some part of your behavior when the person changes his body behavior. That is, every time he blinks, you nod.

6.3.3 Matching Voice Tone

Some people speak in a high-pitched voice; some speak in a very low voice. As much as possible, when you use this skill, match the tone of voice. Of course, be careful not to be mocking or obvious. A slight shift in your voice tone might be enough.

Also, I wouldn't recommend matching every voice tone. For example, if the person is angry or weeping, it would rarely be appropriate for you to match those tones.

You can match various aspects of voice tone, such as pitch, timbre, and emphasis.

6.3.4 Matching Voice Volume

Similar to the previous skill, match the volume or voice level of the person. If they raise the volume of their voice or drop to a whisper, you can adjust the volume of your voice in the same direction.

6.3.5 Matching Grammar or Vocabulary

Erickson was treating a man who came in and exclaimed something like: "I know I ain't no damn good and you most probably won't want to see a goddamned guy like me, but mister, I need some help 'cause I can't no way help myself." He threw some crumpled dollar bills on Erickson's desk, then turned to leave the office.

Erickson replied: "Where the hell are you going? I do the doctorin' around here and you better listen to whatever the hell I say. Now sit yourself down and listen to me, damn it." This is a dramatic example, but you can do something similar to match the person with whom you are working.

I was working with a woman using hypnosis and after she emerged from the trance, she mentioned to me that every time I used the word unconscious (my preferred term), she saw herself being wheeled into the operating theatre having been given drugs to make her unconscious. She preferred the term subconscious. I used that term in subsequent sessions, and this troubling image never reappeared.

Again, it is important to be careful here and not come across as mocking or disrespectful when using this method.

6.4 Guiding Attention and Associations

Whatever you mention might have an influence on the person's thinking, images, and associations. The stories you tell and the words and phrases you use are likely to call forth certain things from the person with whom you are working. So, be careful and be mindful of what you choose to speak about.

For example, if you tell a story about someone getting divorced, you are likely to guide people to think about divorce, either ones that have touched them in the past or the possibility of a current or future divorce.

In contrast, if you mention pleasant memories, people will be more likely to conjure up their own pleasant memories.

In a famous video of Erickson's work *(The Artistry of Milton H. Erickson)*, Erickson mentions to the subject, Mondi, that he was working with a woman a few nights before and she remembered something from the time before she was 5 years old. He then mentions that the woman thought of a happy memory of

a pet she had. Later, Erickson suggests that Mondi remember and revivify an earlier memory. It is no coincidence that Mondi remembers a pleasant memory of a time before she was 5 years old. It even involved animals (she recalls splashing in a pond with ducks).

I often find myself telling stories to a person in trance and notice that I have included details of the story that I have never mentioned before when I have told that particular story. Later the person often reports something significant related to that previously untold detail, so I assume my nonconscious mind has had a sense of what kinds of associations might be helpful to evoke in this person.

What I am suggesting is that you avoid creating associations with unpleasant topics like pain, failure, and the like, unless you have a very deliberate reason for bringing these things into the person's experience.

Hypnotherapist: There are many things you can experience in trance. You might experience time changing in some direction. You know how when you are with friends out to dinner and the conversation is engaging, you might look up after a time and notice all the waiters and the restaurant staff waiting for you to go home. You hadn't even noticed that hours had passed. Perhaps you hadn't even tasted your food. You were just absorbed in the conversation.

In this example, the person would probably be guided to thinking about or remembering friends, food, and restaurants, as well as being invited to time distortion.

6.5 The Confusion Technique

Erickson had the idea that much resistance in hypnosis (and therapy) arises from the conscious mind. When this was interfering, he occasionally used a method he called the confusion technique. He would use a long series of complicated verbalizations that had the ultimate effect of "knocking out" the person's conscious control by overwhelming its processing abilities, thereby letting them more easily go into trance.

He had several methods of doing this, but the easiest to teach is one in which the hypnotist uses two or more pairs of opposite concepts and begins mixing and matching them in various ways.

Let's take the opposites: now/then, forget/remember, and conscious/unconscious.

Hypnotherapist: Now you can be conscious of certain unconscious processes and one could be unconscious about certain conscious things and there are things that one might be conscious of now that then one can forget to remember and can now and then remember to forget. These forgettings can be memorable now, but if I asked you about them later, you might then not remember that you forgot them. That is, consciously, you might not remember but your unconscious mind is likely to remember now what your unconscious forgot then. So, then, how does your unconscious decide what to remember, what to make conscious and what to forget, and what to keep unconscious? I don't really know how to explain it all, but you don't really have to understand. You can just go into trance in the way that is right for you.

Now let's use another set of opposites: you/me, notice/ignore, and this/that.

Hypnotherapist: You can notice what you notice. You may notice you. You may notice me. You may notice me noticing you. You may notice you noticing this or that. This is something you can ignore or attend to. Your unconscious mind can be put on notice to notice this or it can be put on notice to notice that. The me in you and the you in me are interacting in various ways at the conscious and unconscious level. You can notice anything about you or about me that you do and you can also ignore what you notice or attend to what you have been ignoring or will ignore. You might say that ignorance is bliss and maybe not.

The cumulative effect of this series of verbalizations is that the person stops tracking what you are saying consciously and gives up to go into trance.

This can be a tricky, manipulative method, so I suggest you use it sparingly. I only employ it when the person I am working with has a mind that just won't quit and that is getting in the way of his or her going into trance.

Experiment:
Try the Confusion Technique

Come up with your own set of opposite concepts. Start with two pairs. Write them down to help you remember and keep track of them and begin to weave them into a series of statements or questions. You might try writing some things out first or just jump in and start talking. It may take you two or three tries to get the hang of this. Not only is it a skill that you need to develop to use, but it can be confusing for the person who is using the method as well.

The Culture and Territory of Trance Land

In the next set of chapters, we will be detailing the curious language, culture, and landscape of trance land.

We will begin teaching you a dialect called "hypnotic language" so you can easily maneuver in trance land. Next we will visit the territory of Hypnotherapy, the place in which you will learn to use trance to bring about change. Finally, we will visit the territory of Inclusion, which is both a method of hypnosis and a way to use the permissive methods as stand-alone, non-hypnotic methods.

7. The Language of Trance

When I first became a therapist, I learned that one of the skills I needed to develop was the ability to help people get specific and concrete when describing their problem situations. The language of trance is almost a mirror image of this specific and concrete focus.

You need to develop skills like the most abstract and obscure lecturer you have ever heard to master the language of trance. Or think of the most confusing and unspecific friend or acquaintance you have, someone you have trouble understanding.

There is a set of language skills and methods we will examine here. Like any new language, it will probably be a little awkward at first and take some practice. But like any new language, you can learn and master it.

7.1 Use Passive Language

One way to facilitate trance is to use passive language. Writing instructors typically warn writers away from using passive voice, a language form that drops out actors from sentences. "The plates were picked up from the table and put in the sink" is a good example, as it leaves out the person who picked up the dishes. Writing comes more alive when it is written in a more active voice. It is the opposite of this approach to evoking trance. I encourage you to use passive voice. Or to put that last sentence in passive language: You are encouraged to use the passive voice.

7.1.1 Drop the Actor and Willfulness Out of the Sentence

The first way to create passive language is to drop out the actor in the sentence. The second method is to use nominalization, or turning a verb into a noun.

Instead of saying, "You can relax," the passive language way of saying the same thing is "Relaxation can happen." Passive language drops the willfulness from the statement or question. This is important because trance is more of an allowing than a willful, effortful experience.

Hypnotherapist: Many things can occur during trance. Various shifts may happen in your body, in your mind, in your emotions. Noticing these things can just happen or not, but no concern or attention needs to be paid to them if they are not of concern. That's right . . . just allowing . . . whatever happens . . . to unfold in its own way . . . at its own pace.

Hypnotherapist: Attention can wander to the furniture of the room, to the breathing, to the voice, to the wandering thoughts, to the shifting sensations, or anything else that captures the attention.

7.1.2 Turn Verbs into Nouns

Nomalization has a double effect of dropping out the actor as well as making the words very abstract, often leading the person to give up trying to decode specifics. To do this, just think of a verb and make a noun of it, then use it during an induction or trance.

Here are some examples of verbs and the nouns that you could turn them into:

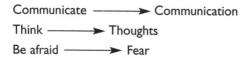

Communicate ⟶ Communication
Think ⟶ Thoughts
Be afraid ⟶ Fear

Hypnotherapist: Communication can occur between the conscious and the unconscious, but awareness doesn't necessarily occur when it happens. Various processes that are part of everyday experience are not always accessible to our awareness, and that is probably generally a good thing. Thoughts drift through the mind and we don't have to attend to them or act on them.

Hypnotherapist: There are thoughts that can come to you in trance, thoughts that you can think, thoughts that can think you. These thoughts can influence feelings, sensations, awarenesses, conclusions, and experiences. You can have thoughts about thoughts, thoughts about feelings, feelings about thoughts, and feelings about feelings.

Hypnotherapist: Fear can be a friend or it can be an enemy. How you relate to fear can change and shift over the course of moments or the course of your life. You can stop and look fear in the eye; you can walk through fear; you can use it as a signal. As Roosevelt said, "The only thing we have to fear is fear itself," which seems like a paradox. You can learn to be comfortable with fear.

7.1.2 Use Empty Words

I sometimes call these words politician or preacher words. Why? Because politicians and preachers are often speaking to a large group of people and they avoid getting too specific to ensure that listeners can make their own meanings (and politicians often don't want to be pinned down to specifics). So, in this method, avoid the use of sensory-specific words and phrases that are easy to pin down to specific times, people, places, actions, or things. Get as vague as possible. Think of how a fairy tale starts: "Long ago, far away, there lived a young man who possessed a curious object and this is the story of what he did and what happened to him as a result. . . ." In the story, this invites us to get involved and use our imaginations to fill in the details. In a trance, empty words invite us to use our imaginations and get more involved in our inner life as well as fill in the blanks with our specific desires and details.

Typical empty phrases and words include: *Many, some, things, various, sometimes, some people,* and *do.*

Hypnotherapist: You can do many things in trance; things that are helpful to you in various ways.

Hypnotherapist: You can go wherever you want or find yourself drifting and do whatever is needed in trance. You don't have to do anything or go anywhere that isn't right for you.

Hypnotherapist: You can visit a particular time and place and I don't even have to know where, specifically, you go.

Hypnotherapist: People often have specific realizations in trance that lead to significant changes in their lives.

8. Everything You Always Wanted to Know About the Nature of Hypnosis but Were Too Deeply in Trance to Ask

In this chapter, I will deviate from the listing and detailing of skills and give you a bird's-eye view of hypnosis: what it is, what it is good for, and what you do during trance to help people realize clinical results. Then we'll go back to breaking down the process into specific skills.

First, how do you recognize that a person is in trance? Well, that is individualized. Everyone may have their own signs, both internal and observable by others, that let you and them know that they are in trance. There are some common indicators, however, and I have listed them below.

8.1 Common Trance Indicators

- Flattening of facial muscles
- Change in skin color
- Immobility or lack of orienting movements
- Decrease in orienting movements
- Limb (hand or arm typically) stays in place (often called catalepsy)
- Changes in blinking and swallowing (either faster or slower)
- Altered breathing and pulse (either faster or slower)
- Jerky motor behavior
- Faraway look
- Fixed gaze
- Changed voice quality
- Time lag in response
- Perseveration of response (for example, the head keeps nodding long after the person has nodded to indicate yes)
- Literalism (for example, if you ask, "Can you tell me your middle name," the person would answer, "Yes, I can.")
- Relaxed muscles (not universal; sometimes people are not relaxed at all in trance)

Subjectively, people often report that they lose track of time, see washes of color (interestingly, often purple, one of Erickson's, and Mesmer's, preferred colors), feel time is slowed down or sped up, lose track of some aspect of their body or physical sensations, feel split off from some part of their experience, or drift from one thought, feeling, or sensation to another, and so on. We'll go more into these subjective shifts in a future section (on trance phenomena).

8.2 Four Doorways Into Altered States

Have you noticed that I haven't defined trance yet? Well, in this section, I'll begin that process. There are many kinds of altered states: meditative states, drug-induced altered states, being lost in a fascinating book or movie, being in a flow state, spiritual ecstasy, and so on. Hypnotic trance is one form of altered state, but they all have some common elements—four, to be precise. I call these the four doorways into trance.

8.2.1 Rhythm

In shamanic ceremonies, altered states are often induced by rhythmic drumming. Something in us seems to respond to rhythm. Perhaps it is our ever-present heartbeat, or that of our mother when we were in her womb, or perhaps the rhythm of our breathing, that lends us to entrainment on rhythm. Whatever it is, regularly repeated rhythms such as music, rocking, regular breathing, sing-song patterns of speaking, and other rhythmic patterns can lull us into altered states.

The ones we most commonly use in this approach to hypnosis are voice rhythms. I trained myself initially to speak only when people exhaled. This slowed me down, gave a cue to the person that some kind of conversation was going on that was different from everyday conversation, and provided a regular rhythm to invite the person into an altered state.

Hypnotherapist: [Watching the person's breathing rise and fall for a time before speaking] And you can . . . [speaking when the person exhales and stopping as soon as the breathing out stops] let yourself . . . just . . . be . . . where you are . . . even if . . .

8.2.2 Defocusing Attention

Another aspect of altered state induction, defocused attention, is akin to listening to a boring lecture or just spacing out while sitting or driving a long distance on a straight highway and finding you haven't noticed the road for a while but your mind was active the whole time. We can invite people to this type of experience through our inductions.

Hypnotherapist: You can recall times when you were just drifting, not thinking of anything in particular. Hypnosis can be just like that. Nothing you need to do, just drifting from one thought to another, from one awareness to another.

8.2.3 Narrowly Focused Attention

It may seem contradictory since the previous aspect of inducing an altered state was defocused attention, but narrowly focusing attention is another doorway into trance. This is akin to listening to a riveting speaker or lecturer, or being very absorbed in a suspenseful novel or movie. When attention narrows, trance can ensue. Classical hypnotists sometimes have people gaze at a specific spot on a wall to narrow attention, but in our approach we are not so directive. We can, however, invite people to this kind of attention by reminding them or by speaking about something that captures their attention.

Hypnotherapist: Sometimes when I listen to music, I become very focused on picking out one of the instruments in the piece, say the bass or the piccolo, and I just follow it through the whole song. Later, I realize that I have been in a kind of a trance. You can go back to a similar experience for you and get that sense of focus to continue to go into trance in a way that's right for you.

8.2.4 Dissociation

Disssociation involves inviting people to experience themselves as divided in some way, often getting the sense that some part of them is acting independently. This often happens spontaneously, but can be invited.

Hypnotherapist: One part of you can listen to what I am saying and one part of you can drift away. My teacher, Dr. Erickson, used to put people in trance and then instruct them to recall the humor of their favorite joke but not the content of the joke. This had the effect of teaching the person that they could access any emotion as it was needed without getting all wrapped up in the content.

Hypnotherapist: One time when I was doing a demonstration of hypnosis in Finland, I asked for four volunteers who understood and spoke English very well to come up to be part of the demonstration. During the trance, I invited people to come out of trance from the neck up and stay in trance from the neck down. After that, I invited them all to experience hand levitation. Later one of the demonstration subjects told me that she realized during the trance that she could no longer understand English but that her body still could. She said that when I had invited the hand levitation, she couldn't understand what I was saying and had to wait for the Finnish translation that was being provided. But her hand began to twitch and move even before she heard the translation, so she knew that her body could still understand English even though her mind couldn't.

There are parts of you that can understand things that other parts don't.

These four factors can be used to induce or invite people into any kind of altered state—I believe they are universal. When used in an interpersonal therapeutic setting, these aspects of altered state induction can be used to create a hypnotic altered state or trance.

8.3 Why Use Trance?

Now let's take up another of the overviews of trance. Why use trance in the first place? Why not just use standard therapy or change methods? The simple answer is that trance can complement usual therapy procedures and methods and can sometimes produce results that those standard methods don't.

What trance is especially good for is influencing and changing automatic experiences, that is, those that are not so readily controlled or created by the person's conscious, willful efforts.

For example, if someone came to me for treatment of migraine headaches, I would be inclined to use hypnosis. Of course, a therapist might use stress reduction methods or some other method that relies on the deliberate efforts of the person, but in my experience, hypnosis can be much more effective in a shorter time than standard therapy methods for this kind of problem, and sometimes it is the only effective method.

Hypnosis is very good at changing automatic symptoms and problems because it is good at evoking automatic (nonconscious) changes. In the next section, we'll discuss how to decide when to use hypnosis and expand on this point.

8.4 When to Use Hypnosis

One time while I was teaching a seminar on hypnosis, someone asked me when in a therapy session I knew I would be using hypnosis with the person. I answered without hesitation: "In the first session; often within the first half of the first session." When trying to explain how I knew so quickly, I discovered that I had a simple criterion for when I use hypnosis and when I don't.

I use hypnosis for nonvoluntary symptoms and problems; that is, those problems that the person cannot produce upon demand. And I don't use hypnosis for problems that can be changed by deliberate efforts, activities, and changes within the person's conscious control.

Of course, there is a problem with this simple criterion: many problems can be viewed as a mix of voluntary and nonvoluntary elements. But most problems are primarily one or the other, so in practice, it is relatively easy for me to decide. And my decision is influenced by how much effort the person (or others, such as medical practitioners) has spent unsuccessfully to treat the problem before he or she came to see me for help. If someone has tried many ways to free himself from panic attacks, such as taking medication, applying methods of cognitive-behavioral therapy, reading self-help books on the subject, and so on, I will be more inclined to use hypnosis. Why? Because reasonable methods of voluntary activity haven't helped.

One could, of course, use a combination of hypnosis and other methods, since many problems are a combination of voluntary and nonvoluntary elements, and that's what I often do. I often use a combination of hypnotic and nonhypnotic interventions.

Let's examine a few common presenting problems for therapists and whether they are voluntary, nonvoluntary, or some combination of both.

8.4.1 Panic Attacks

Panic attacks are typically nonvoluntary, since the feelings and sensations of panic usually arise without people's conscious awareness and, despite their best deliberate efforts, they cannot stop or control the panicked feelings or sensations. Good for trance work.

8.4.2 Smoking

Smoking has a combination of voluntary (buying or borrowing cigarettes, picking up a cigarette and putting it in one's mouth, lighting it up, inhaling) and nonvoluntary (craving nicotine, relaxed feelings after taking a puff) elements. Thus, one might intervene with a combination of hypnosis and nonhypnotic methods.

At a workshop on hypnosis, I happened to mention that the long-term success of hypnosis with smoking cessation was only about 20–25%. During a break, a participant in the workshop told me that he was achieving a greater than 90% success rate using hypnosis with smokers. I asked him to describe his method, so I could try it out. He told me that he advertised in the newspaper for hypnotic treatment to help people stop smoking. When people called, he told them they must prove to him that they were motivated to stop smoking. They could do that by not smoking for three days and then calling him. He offered an appointment for them the very next day. I was amused by this method, since it was obvious to me, but not to him, that he was using a very powerful voluntary intervention for smoking cessation. Anyone who was willing and able to go three days without a cigarette was through the first part of major withdrawal. Then using hypnosis to support them through the next part of smoking cessation became much more successful. He had also weeded out most smokers and therefore worked with a highly select and motivated group. I thought it was somewhat akin to asking people to stop being depressed for three days and then accepting them into treatment for depression.

Voluntary interventions for smokers could involve getting them to wait longer and longer between each cigarette; they could involve holding the cigarette between any other fingers than usual and on the hand in which the smoker didn't usually hold the cigarette; they could involve writing a letter, or making a phone call, or doing some exercise one had been putting off before the next cigarette.

Nonvoluntary (hypnotic) interventions for smoking could involve changes in muscle tension (since people often smoke to relax or relieve tension); changes in blood vessel dilation (since nicotine helps blood vessels dilate, and therefore provides physiological relaxation); changes in cravings (probably related to brain and cell chemistry that are implicated in the addictive side of smoking); and so on.

8.4.3 Insomnia

Again, insomnia is a good subject for trance because it is mainly nonvoluntary. People have typically already tried to make themselves go to sleep and it hasn't worked.

8.4.4 Dissociation

Another good problem for trance is dissociation, since it usually occurs without a person's conscious intention. It feels automatic to most people when it happens. They either don't even notice that it is happening or has happened, or they notice it but can't control it. They just space out or feel detached.

8.4.5 Depression

Depression is usually a combination of actions and nonvoluntary experience. People often withdraw from social connections before or as they begin feeling depressed. They often begin to think in certain ways that support depression. They usually become less physically active. They often focus on their failings or bad things that have happened in the past or could happen in the future. These are all things that they might be able to influence by shifting their thinking, attention, or actions.

The nonvoluntary aspects of depression, often treated with medications, are more amenable to hypnotic intervention. These include brain chemical levels and energy levels. Some people are not helped by medications or only helped a bit, and hypnosis can be a good adjunct or alternative treatment.

8.5 Trance Phenomena

When people go into trance, they regularly have alterations in the areas of perceptions, memory, sensations, physiology, and their sense of time and space, among other changes. These sometimes occur spontaneously and can also be evoked or invited by the hypnotist.

In this section we'll go over the list of the most common of these alterations, usually referred to as trance phenomena or hypnotic phenomena. I'll also discuss how to evoke or invite people to experience them during trance.

What are trance phenomena good for?

- They convince the person and you that the person is in trance.
- They usually deepen the person's involvement in the trance experience.
- They are also used as treatments (we'll discuss this more in a later section).

While trance phenomena can be dramatic, they can also be seen as exaggerated forms of things that occur in less dramatic ways in everyday life. For example, if you work in a hospital, after some time you don't smell the "hospital smell" that is ever-present for visitors. This is an everyday example of the trance phenomenon called *negative hallucination*, that is, not per-

ceiving something that is present in one's sensory experience. Similarly, you might sometimes hear someone calling your name on a crowded street and find that you had imagined it. This is an everyday example of what hypnotists call *positive hallucination*.

You can think of trance in two ways, then. One is that it acts like a magnifying glass for everyday experiences, making them more dramatic. The other analogy I use is that trance allows you to get your hands on the control knob of automatic experiences. It's a bit like those light switches that allow you to dim or brighten a light by turning a knob. Trance allows you to turn the intensity down or up on some parts of experience (again, sensations, perceptions, memory, the automatic parts of physiology, or perceptions of time and space). For example, turning the knob up on memory could create what is called *hypermnesia*—remembering things vividly—while turning down the memory knob could create amnesia—forgetting.

If I suggested to you (in your everyday state of consciousness) that you could experience yourself as being on the other side of the room, you probably wouldn't be able to do that. But if you are in trance and you are invited to that altered sense of the location of your body, you would be more likely to experience it. Trance can make our inner experiences more plastic, more malleable.

What follows is a list of the kinds of areas and changes that can be evoked in the trance state.

Alterations That Make Up Trance Phenomena

Body perception
- Sensations
- Kinesthetic qualities
- Location or position
- Proportion
- Pain or pleasure
- No body

Visual perception
- Integrity of image
- Color
- Size
- Distance
- Edges
- Clarity or blurriness
- No visuals

Auditory perception
- Loudness or softness
- Background or foreground
- Voice or sound quality
- Shifting or substituting sounds
- No sound

Taste and smell perceptions
- Recalling
- Substituting
- Shifting
- Not noticing

Time perception

Time expansion
Time contraction
Age regression
Age progression
No time

Attention

Guiding attention
Diverting attention
Mindful or observer attention
Not attending or noticing

Memory

Amnesia or selective forgetting
Hypermnesia (vivid remembering
   or remembering things one
   had forgotten)
Altered or constructed memories

Physiological shifts

Blood flow
Heart rate
Muscle tension
Body chemicals
Nerve transmission

Muscle movement

Catalepsy
Hand or arm levitation
Automatic or ideomotor movements
   (movements that reflect ideas or thoughts)
Automatic or trance writing

Associations

Dissociation, splitting or making
distinctions

New associations or linkages

Posthypnotic suggestions or links

Emotions

Losing old emotions

Substituting new emotions

No emotions

8.6 Methods for Evoking Trance Phenomena

I will remind you here that you are not adding anything from the outside when you invite people to experience these experiential changes we call *trance phenomena* (or sometimes *hypnotic phenomena*).

These trance phenomena already exist within people as potentials and are evoked by the interactions between hypnotist and client. After many years of doing hypnosis, I still find these manifestations of people's ability to shift their inner experience fascinating. As you witness them, I suspect you will feel the same.

In this section, you will learn five ways to evoke trance phenomena.

8.6.1 Giving Permission

The first way to evoke trance phenomena is to give permission for them to happen, or for a specific one to happen. Often this is all people need to begin the process of evoking automatic changes (or even less than that, at times, since they will happen spontaneously without you mentioning or inviting them).

You use the same permissive methods we discussed in the first part of the book when inducing trance. Remember the two types of permission: *Permission to* and *permission not to have to.* I will illustrate these in the examples below.

Hypnotherapist: Your hand and arm can start to lift up a little at a time without you lifting it.

Hypnotherapist: Time can change. It might become more stretched out, or it might become more condensed, or you could just lose track of time altogether.

Hypnotherapist: You could notice that you are starting to become numb in some places in your body.

Hypnotherapist: You don't have to hear anything that isn't relevant for you.

8.6.2 Presupposing Response

Evoking trance phenomena by presupposing a response uses the same method we discussed earlier in Chapter 2, but this time it is used specifically to evoke the automatic sensory, perceptual, and physiological changes that constitute the trance phenomena.

Hypnotherapist: How quickly will one of those hands lift up?

Hypnotherapist: Which one will lift up first?

Hypnotherapist: What will you notice first that will let you know which hand is going to lift up?

Hypnotherapist: How relaxed will you become? I really don't know.

Hypnotherapist: When will you start to experience that numbness? Your unconscious will decide and let us both know in the appropriate time and way.

8.6.3 Reminding and Guiding Associations to Previous Everyday Experience

It can be helpful to remind people of previous experiences similar to trance phenomena they have had in their lives. This reminder may serve as a mini evocation and lead to more pronounced trance phenomena.

Hypnotherapist: Perhaps you can recall driving down the highway on a long trip; time just disappeared.

Hypnotherapist: When the dentist gave you Novocain, you experienced that numbness. Your body and your unconscious mind can remember that physiologically and experientially and create a similar kind of numbness where you need it now.

8.6.4 Analogies, Anecdotes, and Stories

Using analogies, anecdotes, and stories is a complex skill and we will take it up in a future section as well, but in this approach, we use many stories as a method for inviting change and for evoking automatic changes while the person is in trance. In the

examples that follow, I will add some commentary in italics in the stories to highlight where I am evoking trance phenomena.

Hypnotherapist: When I was a child, I couldn't wait to get out of school at the end of the day. During the last half hour (school let out at 3 in the afternoon), I was a boy divided [*this is an invitation to dissociation*]. One part of my attention was on the clock on the front wall of the classroom; one part of my attention was on the teacher and what she was saying (the penalties were harsh for not attending in my school); and one part of me was already imagining what fun I would have after I was out of this building.

The problem was that the type of industrial clocks we had in our classrooms had a tendency to have the hands stick and stay in place [*this is an invitation to immobility of the hands*]. It seemed like it would be 2:33 for 15 minutes [*this is an invitation to time distortion*]. That hand just wouldn't move. Finally it would jump up and move 2 or 3 minutes at a time [*this is an invitation to hand levitation*].

Hypnotherapist: I was on an airplane coming back to the United States from Australia a few years ago. When we crossed the International Date Line, the captain came on the intercom and announced, "In 2 minutes, it will be yesterday." That made me realize that clock and calendar time can be different from subjective time. You can change time inside so that you have enough time to sort out everything that needs to be sorted out. And you can transport yourself to any time you need to visit, the past or the future, to resolve what needs to be resolved.

8.6.5 Interspersed Phrases

Again, we have covered the use of interspersed phrases in an earlier section, but not the application of the method to evoke trance phenomena. As a reminder, interspersal involves empha-sizing certain phrases and words nonverbally to evoke a non-conscious response. The bold phrases and words in the follow-ing examples relate to trance phenomena.

(To evoke hand and arm levitation to the face)

Hypnotherapist: I **moved** houses last year. Many things **changed** when I moved. All those **changes** took some getting used to. Some of them were **uplifting** and some were challeng-

ing. I had to **face** some issues within myself and get in **touch** with strengths and vulnerabilities that I wasn't so aware of before. Looking back, I know I made some personal growth and **movement**. We some-times **make progress** through challenges and difficulties.

Hypnotherapist: You can go **back** to a time when you were **relaxed** and felt **better**. You came to me looking for **relief** and I would like you to **find**

relief and **feel better**. In fact, it might seem close to impossible, but I would like you to **feel good**. It's hard to tell whether there is something in the **muscles** that could **change** to help you **feel better** or something else. Either way, your unconscious has your **back** and can help you **make changes** that will **resolve** things.

9. The $64,000 Question: What Do You Do Once the Person Is in Trance to Get the Clinical Result?

How I wish someone had answered this $64,000 question for me during my training in hypnosis and hypnotherapy. I learned a lot about getting a person into trance, handling abreactions, and giving suggestions, but little about the actual nitty-gritty of facilitating change with hypnotherapy if simple suggestion did not produce results (it often doesn't, in my experience).

So here, for much less than $64,000, is my answer.

9.1 Goals of Traditional Versus Solution-Oriented Hypnosis

In the solution-oriented approach to hypnotherapy, the goals of treatment are substantially different from traditional hypnotherapeutic (or even nonhypnotic therapy) approaches.

Traditional hypnotherapy tries to find sources or causes of problems through hypnosis. Since hypnosis is thought to directly access repressed unconscious knowledge or information, it is used to discover or uncover hidden, nonobvious causes, traumas, or early life decisions (such as "I will never trust anyone" or "I have to be quiet or I will be hurt") for current problems.

Embedded in this traditional approach is another idea: that people are flawed and pathological due to some personality, emotional, neurological, or trauma-based problems or deficits. Hypnotherapy is designed to correct or compensate for these problems or deficits.

Ericksonian or solution-oriented hypnosis holds no such assumption of pathology, problem, damage, or deficit. Instead, we are oriented to people's abilities and resources. Therefore, we use the hypnotic process to discover and connect to resources.

Another difference is in the time orientation of the solution-oriented approach versus the traditional. We are oriented more to the present and future in this approach, whereas traditional approaches are more oriented to the past and its relationship to the present.

Of course, sometimes in the trances that occur in this approach, people do uncover or discover some previously unknown or unacknowledged information related to their problems, but the hypnotherapist does not guide people to the past in order to discover these things.

The rest of this chapter will show, in more specific ways, how we implement this different orientation in hypnotherapy.

9.2 Class of Problems and Class of Solutions Model

Erickson could be a mystery to those who studied his work. He seemed to be endlessly creative in his clinical work, rarely using the same approach to the same problem, even when he had been successful with that approach in previous cases. He approached every person as a unique individual and delighted in creating a particular intervention for that person or clinical situation.

Most therapists do not operate in this way. We learn theories and a set of interventions we try to personalize, but we generally do not make up a whole new approach for each person.

But there was a pattern to Erickson's interventions. One must look deeper to find it. I have created a model that has helped me and others to understand how Erickson generated new interventions for each person and that has helped those who have used the model to do the same for their clients and patients. I call this model the class of problems and class of solutions model. I had a flash of insight one day while reading about a case of Erickson's. He wasn't focused on working on the specific presenting problem directly (he is often referred to as an indirect hypnotherapist). Instead he seemed to move to another level and abstract the kind or type of problem that included the particular problem. This gave him a lot of options for intervention and ensured that he wouldn't have to repeat himself.

For example, if the presenting problem was impotence, one class of problems to which it could belong is "lack of blood flow." Now, you may notice I wrote "to which it could belong," and this indicates something that allows for even more flexibility. There is not necessarily one class of problems. That is, the particular problem must fit with the class, but there may be multiple classes to which the problem could belong. In the case of impotence, the class of problems might be anxiety or performance anxiety. Or it could be low levels of sex hormones. Or it could be relationship problems.

Whatever class of problems you determine would fit, the next step is to come up with a class of solutions that could potentially resolve that problem. This is where this Ericksonian or solution-oriented approach really differs from traditional hypnotherapy. In this approach, we search for resources (in the automatic realm) that could be used to shift the problem. We are not searching for past traumas or decisions that created the problem. We are not looking for underlying, hidden motivations or issues that are not obvious to the client or patient. We are simply focused on the presenting complaint and marshaling the resources needed to resolve or shift it.

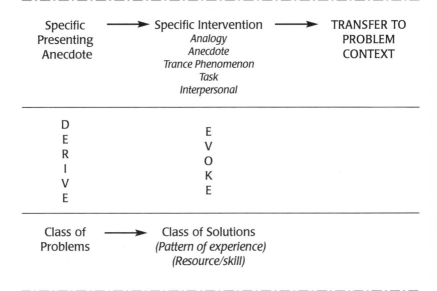

What follows is a detailed set of instructions for implementing the class of problems and class of solutions model in hypnotherapy settings. One could use it in nonhypnotic settings, of course, but then the focus would not typically be on evoking automatic or nonconscious resources and abilities. One could also use it in nontherapy settings, but that is far beyond the scope of this book.

9.2.1 Determine the Focus for the Hypnotic Intervention

Obviously, for this model to lend itself to hypnosis, the problem must be cast in terms of an automatic process. For that to happen, one has to get a clear, specific problem to focus upon. Some therapists are used to being more vague about the goals of hypnosis or therapy. Not here. No "working through emotional issues" or "uncovering insights into self-sabotaging." These problems are more like "migraine headaches," or "panic attacks." If you can't get specific or if focusing on specific presenting problems is anathema to you, this model will not serve you well. There is a relatively easy way to determine the focus for treatment in most cases: pay attention to what people are complaining about when they seek treatment, and use that as the focus. Unless people have been well trained by previous therapists, they rarely arrive in treatment asking for help with their unresolved oedipal conflicts, uncathected emotions, a wounded inner child, or even traumas. They mention specific problems that are bringing suffering to their lives: insomnia, flashbacks to traumatic events, depressed feelings, chronic pain in some part of their body, impotence or lack of sexual desire, an unreasonable fear of something that limits them in their lives, and so on. It is one of these specific complaints that we use as a starting point for this model. Stay close to the presenting complaint or problem when devising an intervention using this model.

9.2.2 Turn Problems Into Processes

To get this model to work, one must then turn the problem
into a process. It must have aspects that are open to change.
Sometimes this means there is a sequence of things that happen automatically that we
could intervene in. Sometimes
this means that we are merely
casting the problem as something that gets re-created
again and again; thus it is open
to change by getting something else to happen instead.

For example, a migraine
headache can be viewed as
having a number of elements
that might lend themselves to
intervention and change.
Some blood vessels dilate and some contract. There is a change
in blood chemistry. Muscles tense in certain parts of the body.
Ears often become more sensitive to sounds; eyes become
more sensitive to light. There are often sensations or visual dis-
tortions that precede the development of a migraine (so-called
prodromal symptoms). Interventions (derived from classes of
solutions) could be targeted at any of these aspects of the
process or pattern of the migraine.

Don't think of the problem as a thing, but as a set of internal
actions (mostly automatic and outside the person's conscious
control or even awareness, of course; that is why we are using
trance). Choose one or more of those actions and intervene in
them to discover if trance can make a positive difference.

9.2.3 How Does the Person (or Body) Do This Problem?

One of the ways to get to the process description is to ask yourself: If I had control over this person's physical, physiological, sensory, or emotional systems, how would I create this problem? For example, one could create a good panic attack by increasing the person's heart rate, and creating sweaty palms, racing thoughts, and images or thoughts of terrible things like heart attacks or bad things happening to people or their loved ones. Each of these things can be mapped onto the class of problems and class of solutions template.

9.2.4 What Class of Problem Could It Belong To?

From the description of process, one can derive a class of problems to which a particular problem could belong. Using the panic attack example above, one class of problem could be increased heart rate.

For a person who has been having extramarital affairs, the class of problems could be being impulsive. For someone who suffers from a hair-trigger temper, the class of problems could be "letting feelings cause one's actions." Any class of problem that you can derive from the specific problem at hand will work (as long as you have an idea of its opposite and that it can be changed by hypnosis).

9.2.5 What Is an Opposite Class That Could Solve It?

The next step is to think of the opposite of the class of problems: some resource, skill, pattern of experience, and so forth that could undo the problem. In the example of panic attacks and increased heart rate, the opposite could be decreased or slower heart rate.

9.2.6 What Anecdote, Analogy, Trance Phenomenon, Task Assignment, or Interpersonal Move Could Evoke the Resource?

The next step is to do some intervention that could access or evoke the resource, skill, or pattern of experience that fits with the class of solution. Again, following the above example of decreased heart rate to help stop or reduce panic attacks, you could tell a story about someone who had a reduced heart rate, or use an analogy of turning down the intensity of a light with a dimmer switch, or evoke reduced heart rate as a trance phenomenon. Causing someone to blush due to something you said is an example of an interpersonal move evoking the resource.

9.2.7 Transfer the Evoked Ability or Resource to the Problem Area

Transferring evoked resources to the problem is commonly called posthypnotic suggestion, but since I deemphasize the suggestive aspect of hypnosis, let's just call it "linking the evoked resource to the problem area." In essence, what I am suggesting here is that you make some sort of verbal linkage between the ability, skill, pattern of experience, or resource that has been evoked through the intervention (a story, an analogy, a trance phenomenon, an interpersonal move, or a task assignment) and the potential recurrence of the problem.

Hypnotherapist: The next time you would have had a migraine headache, your unconscious mind and your body could work together to shift the blood vessels so that migraines do not occur.

Hypnotherapist: If your unconscious detects any increase in your heart rate that would have led to a panic attack in the past, your body can automatically decrease your heart rate.

This class of problems and class of solutions model may seem a bit complicated at first, but once you get the hang of it, it can help you generate endless interventions. So, please stick with it long enough to master it.

9.3 To Trust Your Unconscious or Not; That is the Question

Dr. Erickson was fond of saying, "Trust your unconscious. It knows more than you do." Erickson held the view that the unconscious was a repository of skills, abilities, and resources. He had a rather positive view compared to Freud's view of the unconscious as a cauldron of repressed and primitive urges that needed the ego and superego to keep it in check, or we would all be Mr. Hydes running around being violent and acting out our selfish needs.

Having been influenced by Erickson, I subscribed to this more benevolent, resourceful view of the unconscious for years. But several things got me to rethink it. First, my good friend and fellow Erickson student, Stephen Gilligan, once gave a session at one of the Erickson conferences titled *If the Unconscious Is So Smart, Why Do People Have Problems or Symptoms?* I thought that was a very good question and it got me thinking.

Some time later, Joe Barber, another colleague, was ranting during our lunch at one of the Erickson conferences, "These Ericksonians are driving me mad running around saying 'Trust your unconscious'! Don't they know the unconscious is dumb, dumb, dumb?"

I considered this dilemma for some years and finally came to a conclusion as to what my view on the matter was. Here's my answer:

The unconscious is smart about what it is smart about, dumb about what it is dumb about and smart about, some things it's dumb to be smart about.

Lest you think I'm just being a smart aleck or trying to use Erickson's confusion technique on you, let me explain.

Let's say you have mastered the sport of tennis. For some time, you've been playing tennis, taking lessons, practicing your swings, your serves, and so on. You're getting pretty good at it. At a certain point, your muscles begin to learn tennis and you don't have to think about it. In fact, you find that if you think about it, you play more poorly. One way to talk about this is to say that your unconscious is smart about playing tennis. You could go out on the court and trust your unconscious, since it knows a lot and has it encoded automatically.

I play guitar and I am pretty good at it. I could give a professional talk, watch television, or read a book and play quite complex things on a guitar at the same time. My fingers know the patterns and I don't have to give it much conscious attention. My unconscious is smart about playing guitar.

So, if your unconscious is smart about something, trust your unconscious. But there are some things you shouldn't trust your unconscious about, because your unconscious is dumb about those things. If you don't know touch typing, look at the keys; otherwise your typing will come out like gobbledygook. Your unconscious is dumb about touch typing. I couldn't read a book or give a lecture while I played the mandolin. My unconscious is dumb about playing the mandolin.

Now here's where it gets interesting, especially for hyp-notherapy. Sometimes your unconscious is smart about things it is dumb to be smart about. We know the brain gets grooved in patterns after repeating some experiences. ("Neurons that fire together wire together" is the neurologist's phrase for this). Throughout our lives we sometimes develop unconscious or automatic patterns that no longer serve, or aren't flexible enough to function well, in our current environments.

For example, say someone was sexually abused regularly when she was younger. She used a handy coping mechanism, dissociation, when she was overwhelmed with the emotions or sensations during the sexual abuse. One of my clients told me she would go into a painting hanging on the wall of her bed-room during her abuse.

But that person grows up, moves on a bit, and meets some-one she loves and would like to be close to. She might discover that each time her partner approaches her sexually or even with affectionate touch, without her conscious intention, she dissociates. Her unconscious is smart about dissociating but in this context it is dumb to be smart about that.

That leads to one of the things that hypnosis can contribute to therapy, and this is the heart of the matter. Through hypnosis, we can get access to the nonconscious or automatic patterns the unconscious is smart about and rearrange the wiring. We can undo previous associations and automatic patterns and encourage new associations and patterns.

Sometimes I think of hypnosis as a way to get back to potentials and what the Zen practitioners call "the beginner's mind." It is a chance to start again and update with new flexibilities that can be responsive to current and future realities.

So, to conclude this little but all-important section, trust your unconscious when it is smart about something that works for you in your current life and reality; don't trust your unconscious if it is not smart or automatically skilled in that area; and don't trust your unconscious if what your unconscious mind is smart about and has on automatic pilot is not serving you well or is creating suffering in your current circumstances.

See, that was clear enough, huh? Or clearly confusing if you didn't follow it. If I lost you, go back and read this section again. It is clear, I promise, and it is important for you to understand it in order to use what follows.

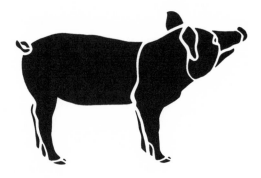

A Guide to Trance Land

9.4 How to Use This Knowledge to Do Hypnotherapy

How can you use the ideas I have discussed to do hypnotherapy? Two ways: Identify the unwanted or unhelpful automatic patterns that are leading to problems; and then introduce changes by splitting and linking, akin to rewiring people's experiential lives. Let's discuss these two ways in more detail.

9.4.1 Find the Place Where Automatic Patterns Occur and Lead to Unwanted Results

Automatic patterns with bad results is the place where the unconscious is smart about things it's dumb to be smart about. The unconscious has gotten skilled at creating, for example, migraine headaches or panic attacks.

So, your task is to identify the patterns and processes that are occurring automatically and leading to problems and then intervene. How do you intervene? By using splitting and linking. Remember, we used these skills to create trance; now we are using them to create therapeutic change.

9.4.2 Introduce Changes Into the Automatic Pattern by Splitting and Linking

I sometimes think of the process of introducing changes as doing plumbing or rewiring on an old house. I come to my client's "house" (the inner life) and discover that some of the old wiring is creating leaks, flooding, power outages, or surges. My job is to rearrange things so that they are "up to code"—that is, so they work well now and in the future.

For example, seeing needles no longer needs to be connected with fear or tense muscles. It can be connected to being healthy, feeling calm, or just watching the needle with no emotional reaction. It has been wired to fear or tense muscles, but hypnosis is an opportunity to rewire, and to rewire without the person having to make any deliberate efforts.

How do we accomplish this rewiring? The ways we have discussed above: evoking abilities or experiences and linking them to other experiences or cues. New associations can be created through trance using stories, permissive suggestions, interspersal, analogies, or trance phenomena.

As a reminder, here is a chart that summarizes typical ways to evoke automatic responses through trance.

How to Evoke Automatic Responses: Trance, Trance Phenomena, and Experiential Shifts

- Reminders of past or everyday experiences that are minor versions of trance phenomena or trance
- Permission
- Possibilities
- Stories or analogies
- Enhancement and encouragement once a little response happens

9.4.3 Settings and Props

Imagine that you were putting on a play and had to populate the stage with items and sets that would evoke the scenes you were trying to get people to envision. Since you can't put everything on stage (it would be too crowded or expensive), you would have to choose some key items that would be most evocative, say a couch here, a telephone there, and so on. Stories are similar. Since you don't have all the time in the world (people would get bored with too much description of setting and props), you must be careful to put in just enough and not too much. This balance usually comes with practice.

9.5 Stories in Trance Work

One way to evoke classes of solutions and resources is to tell stories. I discussed stories a bit earlier, but here I would like to go into more detail. I write stories for a living that are interspersed in my books, and I tell stories in my workshops and seminars, so I have been thinking about what makes an engaging, effective story for some time.

Here is my quick guide to elements of effective, engaging stories. Mastering the art of storytelling can make your hypnotherapy more successful.

9.5.1 Elements of Stories

Some key aspects of the Ericksonian approach are storytelling in therapy and trancework.

I was not a natural or comfortable storyteller and had to deliberately learn and practice storytelling. To make this skill more available to you, I will detail some of the elements of effective storytelling.

9.5.2 Characters

Part of what hooks us into stories is that they have characters (often people, but sometimes animals or inanimate objects we bring to life) with whom we can identify. These characters can evoke empathy and emotions in us when we imagine ourselves as them.

So, ensure that there are characters in the stories you tell during trance.

9.5.3 Action

What makes a story different from an analogy is that something happens during a story while an analogy is merely a static description.

Years ago, during a therapy session in which the mother in the family we were seeing literally would not stop talking, my cotherapist said to our primary client, "Your mother has a freeway mouth with no on-ramp." That image is an analogy. His

point was that, since no one in the session could get a word in edgewise due to the mother's non-stop talking, she was like a highway which nobody could get on.

To turn it into a story, he might have said, "I live in Casa Grande and one day, when I went to get onto the freeway to go to Tempe, I found the only freeway on-ramp was closed for repair. I was stumped and sat in my car by the closed entrance for some time pondering my dilemma. How was I to get to Tempe? Finally I realized that there must have been a way to get there from Casa Grande before the freeway was built, so I looked on a map I had in the car and found another route, which actually turned out to be very scenic and interesting, although it did take a bit longer."

Now this is a story since something happened in it.

9.5.4 Beginnings, Middles, and Ends

One of the things that happened in the story above is that it had a beginning (he went to the freeway and couldn't get on); a middle (he sat in his car and was stumped); and an ending (he had a realization, then consulted a map and found another way to Tempe).

Some people who aren't good joke tellers or storytellers often leave out one of these crucial elements, and the story falls apart or becomes less compelling.

9.5.5 Dialogue

Including exact wording and quotations is another way to bring stories alive. If you merely describe what went on (they yelled at each other for a while), it is typically less compelling than giving actually dialogue ("I'll never trust you again," she said. "You won't have to because I am leaving and you'll never see me again," he responded.) In trance, of course, dialogue gives you an opportunity for interspersal as well (He told her, "Just make yourself comfortable.").

9.5.6 Suspense and Engagement of Interest

Make your stories interesting enough for people to care and be curious about what happens in them and to the characters. Trance gives even more opportunity for suspense, since we often pause to match the breath and this sometimes leaves the listener curious a bit longer than in the usual telling of a tale.

People get engaged when a character is in danger, confusion, or conflict, so including any of these elements can raise the suspense and engagement levels.

9.5.7 Vague Enough to Allow for Identification and Imagination

Think of how a fairy tale starts, as I mentioned earlier in the book: "Long ago, far away, there lived a young man who possessed a curious object. This is the story of what happened to him and how he learned the true nature of the object that was to change his life."

In my English class, they called this "climbing the ladder of abstraction" (see, I was paying attention). The more vague you can be, the more abstract the words and phrases, the more listeners are compelled to fill in the details with their imaginations. This element uses a skill we discussed in an earlier section on empty words.

9.5.8 Enough Specific Details

At the same time, too much vagueness might make the story too boring or not give the listener enough to hang onto. So, just as in using dialogue, put in enough specifics to give the person something to relate to. Include names, places, particular actions, sensory details using any or all of the senses, and so on.

10. Inclusion as Intervention

After using the solution-oriented approach to hypnosis for a while, some of the people with whom I worked starting remarking that the induction itself was healing for them even before I got into the actual intervention and treatment parts of the trance.

One day a particular person mentioned that she had been to see a previous therapist who used hypnosis to treat her post-traumatic problems related to her experience of child sexual abuse. She said, "I like the kind of trance you do better than the type he used." When I pressed her for more about that, she said: "He did working trances. I would go back to the past and reexperience the abuse. I felt exhausted and upset after each session. But I thought that's what I needed to do to get better. You do healing trances. I don't have to do anything; just be. At the end of those trances, something has changed and I feel better, more integrated."

After hearing that, I realized that there was something inherent in the very permissive approach that was healing, and I began to be more deliberate about both using and articulating the permissive aspects of the work. I started calling this inclusive therapy. (I have written a whole book on the subject,

A Guide to Inclusive Therapy, also published by W. W. Norton, if you'd like to delve more into it.)

There are two main aspects of inclusive therapy: *permission* and *inclusion*. I find them to be helpful for many people, but especially helpful for people who present with dissociation, shame, borderline issues, and posttraumatic problems.

10.1 Permission

The first element of inclusive therapy is permission. As in the induction part of this approach, we give people permission to experience whatever they are experiencing or will experience. This is why the approach is often helpful with shame issues. ("I shouldn't feel this way or I must be this way" or "I won't be okay.")

There are two kinds of permission: *permission to* and *permission not to have to.*

The phrases that are used include: "It's okay to ... ", "You can ... ", "You don't have to ... ", "It's okay if you don't ... "

Here are a few examples of using this as treatment:

Hypnotherapist: It's okay to be numb and not to feel anything in that area. It may change over time and it doesn't have to change or change quickly.

Hypnotherapist: It makes sense that you would be feeling frightened about getting close to someone. It doesn't mean that fear will be there forever and it is okay to feel it now.

Hypnotherapist: You don't have to know right now. It's okay not to know. You don't have to be better right now.

10.2 Inclusion of Opposites

The second element of inclusion taps into the nonrational aspects of trance: allowing two seeming opposites at the same time in one's experience. This is in large part why inclusion can be helpful for those displaying or experiencing border-line issues, which often manifest as ambiva-lence (*I Hate You, Don't Leave Me* is the title of a popular book on bor-derlines). The conscious rational mind tends to think in either/or or this/but that ways, while inclusion invites a both/and mind-set.

Hypnotherapist: You can be frightened and calm at the same time.

Hypnotherapist: You can be exactly where you are and you can move ahead.

Hypnotherapist: You can want to stay the same and want to change. You can be afraid of changing and you can change.

Hypnotherapist: You may never get over it and you may move on.

Hypnotherapist: You can hold on to let go.

Erickson often used oxymorons to capture this dual experi-ence and make room for it. A person whose parents spoiled him might be told:

Hypnotherapist: Your parents were **awfully good** to you. They were **terribly kind**.

Or a person who was suffering from posttraumatic stress (often characterized by hypervigilance) could be told:

Hypnotherapist:: You can have an **unconcerned vigilance** to interpersonal dangers.

10.3 Identifying Injunctions That Could Yield to Inclusion

Where can you most fruitfully apply inclusion as a treatment in hypnotherapy? When there is ambivalence and where there are what transactional analysis calls *injunctions*. Injunctions are those rules (shoulds and shouldn'ts) that we often pick up from our cultures, our gender training, our parents and families, or decisions we make. ("I'll never be hungry again," vows Scarlett O'Hara.)

Injunctions, like permissions, come in two forms: have to/should/ must and can't/won't/shouldn't.

If you can discern one of these rules that is dominating your client, come up with the opposite permission that might help undo the compulsion to live out the rule.

Hypnotherapist: I know in your family, the rule was always to keep the peace, and sometimes it is okay to rock the boat a little.

Hypnotherapist: In your house, no one was to notice the elephant in the living room, and now that you are an adult, it is okay to notice and speak up about the elephant.

Hypnotherapist: You don't always have to be the nice guy. It's okay to ask for what you want or get angry.

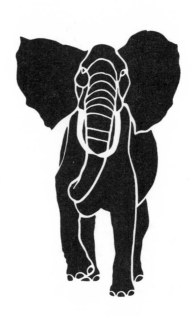

A Guide to Trance Land

11. The Hitchhiker's Guide to Solution-Oriented Hypnosis

Okay, now it might be helpful to give you an overview and review of the process of solution-oriented or Ericksonian hypnosis—let you see the forest after hanging out in the trees for so long. Here is the most succinct overview I can give you, distilling the process into six steps. I named it after one of my favorite books (*The Hitchhiker's Guide to the Galaxy*, the motto of which is "Don't Panic").

Step 1: Take off the pressure and validate the person where he or she is and will be

Give people permission to feel, think, and experience whatever they are and what they might be in the future.

Hypnotherapist: You can just let yourself be where you are. If you are nervous, that's okay. You don't have to be relaxed to be inside. You don't have to listen to or believe everything I say.

If clients respond in some way or do something that they might think is wrong or distracting, validate it and include it in the experience.

Hypnotherapist: That's right. You can open your eyes whenever you want and look around. You may want to close them again or just leave them open and stay in trance, whatever is more comfortable for you.

Step 2: Get rhythm

Speak only when the person exhales. Even if you skip a breath or two, start speaking again on the exhalation.

Step 3: Create an expectancy for responding to the experience and suggestion

Presume that the person will get into the experience and will get the intended results.

Hypnotherapist: I don't know how quickly or deeply you will go inside. Each person is different.

Hypnotherapist: You may or may not notice when you first start to relax more and feel more comfortable.

Step 4: Suggest some automatic changes

Hypnotherapist: Your hand may start to lift up automatically, just a bit at a time.

Hypnotherapist: You may be experiencing some numbness in some part of your body. That numbness could increase until you really notice it.

Step 5: Once you get a response, validate, extend and direct the change towards the clinical goal

Hypnotherapist: And as that hand lifts up, you can be going deeper inside and getting ready to relax even more. Your body can prepare to control the bleeding so that you have just enough to clean out the area and no unnecessary bleeding.

Step 6: Invite the person to reorient to external reality and suggest future positive results

Hypnotherapist: Now at your own rate and pace, you can come back from that inner focus and reorient all the way, bringing with you relaxation and the ability to control your discomfort. You can continue to eliminate any unnecessary discomfort and attend only to the necessary pain.

12. Bad Trance/Good Trance

Here's another concept you might find useful in thinking about hypnosis and hypnotherapy. Several writers have observed that hypnotic trance shows some marked similarities to some types of psychological or mental disturbances, like dissociative disorders and psychotic disorders. There is some truth to this view, and it makes one wonder: Why do these pathological symptoms feel subjectively disturbing and often lead to social and even legal problems for the person who experiences them, while people in trance often express a sense of delight at their experiences in trance?

One way to think about this difference is that there are "symptom trances" and healing trances (or bad trances and good trances). The subjective phenomena are similar but the underlying sensibility is quite different.

What distinguishes a bad trance from a good one? I suggest that one of the main differences is the experience of invalidation versus the experience of validation. In healing trances, we hypnotherapists are providing a validating and accepting relationship (I have to say, especially in this solution-oriented variety, in which validation, permission, and acceptance are such a cornerstone). In bad trance people are routinely invalidated by their contexts and other people (or even themselves through self-doubt and self-criticism).

This is just an idea, but others (see the bibliography in this chapter) have explored the notion in different ways. Many have noted the similarity of trance experiences and psychotic or dissociative problems. Others have linked bad trance to family dysfunction and even torture. If this idea intrigues you, you might read their books to go more in depth on this subject.

I think of hypnotherapy as a way of shifting bad trances to good or healing ones. Below is a chart comparing and contrasting them.

SYMPTOMATIC TRANCE ⟶ HEALING TRANCE

Symptom Induction	Healing Induction
• Invalidation; blame; violating boundaries	• Validation; permission; respecting boundaries
• Mystification; binds; double binds	• Possibility words and phrases
• Coalitions; secrets; negative dissociation	• Helpful distinctions
• Predictions of failure or trouble; threats	• Posthypnotic suggestions; presuppositions of health and healing
• Rigid role assignment; mind reading	• Positive attributions; avoidance of intrusive interpretations
• Repetition of negative experiences, injurious or self-injurious behavior	• Opening of possibilities for changes in experience or behavior
• Negative injunctions (You can't, you shouldn't, you will, you are)	• Empowering and permissive affirmations (You can, it's okay, you may, you could, you have the ability to, you don't have to)
• Repression; amnesia	• Reversible forgetting and remembering
Symptomatic trance is repetitive, self-devaluing, and closes down possibilities. It is a repetition of past states of being that are not updated to fit with current contexts. Self as more than symptom is forgotten.	**Healing trance** is validating, empowering, and opens up possibilities. It is responsive to current contexts. Self as more than symptom is remembered.

Bad Trance/Good Trance Bibliography

Araoz, Daniel. (1984). *The new hypnosis*. New York: Brunner/Mazel.

Beahrs, John. (1982). *Unity and multiplicity*. New York: Brunner/Mazel.

Bliss, Eugene. (1986). *Multiple personality, allied disorders and hypnosis*. New York/Oxford: Oxford University Press.

Gilligan, Stephen. (1987). *Therapeutic trances*. New York: Brunner/Mazel.

Haley, Jay. (1963). *Strategies of psychotherapy*. New York: Grune and Stratton.

Ritterman, Michele. (1983). *Using hypnosis in family therapy*. San Francisco: Jossey-Bass.

Wolinsky, Stephen. (1991). *Trances people live: Healing approaches in quantum psychology*. Falls Village, CT: The Bramble Co.

13. The Process of Ericksonian Hypnotherapy

Here is another overview that may help you get a bird's-eye view of the process of offering hypnotherapy using this orientation.

1. Assess the complaints and identify the goals. Seed changes and create an expectancy for change.

2. Determine that the complaint is an automatic process. (If it is not, pursue nonhypnotic interventions.)

3. Introduce the notion of inner work and hypnosis. Reassure and reframe if necessary.

4. Induce an inner focus, evoke resources, get responses, and help the person rearrange his or her experiential reality (splitting, linking, altering, deleting, and creating sensations and perceptions, and physiological, muscular, psychological, or emotional experiences). Offer a series of possibilities and notice which ones the person responds to.

5. Link evoked resources and alterations to the future and to appropriate contexts.

6. Complete the inner work or hypnosis.

7. Discuss the experience as much or as little as the person

wants. Normalize and reassure if necessary. Continue seeding changes and creating expectancies for change.

8. At the next contact, gather information on postsession response and results and utilize those.

9. Induce the inner state. Continue or expand the responses that helped. Offer new possibilities if necessary.

10. Repeat steps 7–9 as often as necessary until both you and the client are certain you are complete. By complete, I mean that both you and the client are satisfied that all the relevant concerns have been addressed.

11. Arrange for follow-up through scheduled visits, postcards, letters, phone calls, and so on.

Envoi: Leaving Trance Land

Okay, together we have taken a tour of trance land. Having used hypnosis in therapy for over 30 years, I am still learning more about it and hope to keep learning more in the years to come.

From my wanderings in this land, I have tried, through this book, to give you a map to find your way around. I hope I have made the tour sufficiently simple and empowering, so you now feel you can find your way on your own.

I have actually learned more from the people with whom I have worked (commonly called subjects or clients but I prefer to think of them as people) than from any books or courses, but those books and courses got me started and gave me enough confidence to let people teach me. I hope this book has done the same for you.

Trancendentally yours,

Bill

Ericksonian Bibliography

BOOKS BY MILTON H. ERICKSON, MD

COLLECTED PAPERS

Haley, Jay (Editor). *Advanced techniques of hypnosis and therapy: Selected papers of Milton H. Erickson, M.D.* New York: Grune and Stratton, 1967.

Rossi, Ernest L. (Editor). *The Collected papers of Milton Erickson on hypnosis.* New York: Irvington, 1980.

COAUTHORED BOOKS

Cooper, Linn, and Erickson, Milton H. *Time distortion in hypnosis.* New York: Irvington, 1982.

Erickson, Milton H., Hershmn, Seymour, and Secter, Irving I. *The practical application of medical and dental hypnosis.* Chicago: Seminars on Hypnosis Publishing, 1981.

Erickson, Milton H., Rossi, Ernest L., and Rossi, Sheila I. *Hypnotic realities: The induction of clinical hypnosis and forms of indirect suggestion.* New York: Irvington, 1976.

Erickson, Milton H., and Rossi, Ernest L. *Hypnotherapy: An exploratory casebook.* New York: Irvington, 1979.

Erickson, Milton H., and Rossi, Ernest L. *Experiencing hypnosis: Therapeutic approaches to altered states.* New York: Irvington, 1981.

Erickson, Milton H., and Rossi, Ernest L. *The February man: Evolving consciousness and identity in hypnotherapy.* New York: Brunner/Mazel, 1989.

BOOKS EDITED BY OTHERS

(PRIMARILY CONSISTING OF ERICKSON'S MATERIAL)

Haley, Jay. *Conversations with Milton H. Erickson, M.D. Volume I: Changing individuals; Volume II: Changing couples; Volume III: Changing children and families.* New York: Triangle (Norton), 1985.

Havens, Ronald. *The wisdom of Milton H. Erickson.* New York: Irvington, 1984.

O'Hanlon, William H., and Hexum, Angela L. *An uncommon casebook: The complete clinical work of Milton H. Erickson.* New York: Norton, 1990.

Rosen, Sidney. *My voice will go with you: The teaching tales of Milton H. Erickson.* New York: Norton, 1982.

Rossi, Ernest L., and Ryan, Margaret O. *Life reframing in hypnosis: The seminars, workshops and lectures of Milton H. Erickson, Volume II.* New York: Irvington, 1985.

Rossi, Ernest L., and Ryan, Margaret O. *Mind-body communication in hypnosis: The seminars, workshops and lectures of Milton H. Erickson, Volume III.* New York: Irvington, 1986.

Rossi, Ernest L., and Ryan, Margaret O. *Creative Choice in Hypnosis: The Seminars, Workshops and Lectures of Milton H. Erickson, Volume IV.* New York: Irvington, 1991.

Rossi, Ernest L., Ryan, Margaret O., and Sharp, Florence A. *Healing in Hypnosis: The Seminars, Workshops and Lectures of Milton H. Erickson, Volume I.* New York: Irvington, 1983.

Zeig, Jeffrey K. *A teaching seminar with Milton H. Erickson.* New York: Brunner/Mazel, 1980.

Zeig, Jeffrey K. *Experiencing Erickson: An introduction to the man and his work.* New York: Brunner/Mazel, 1985.

BOOKS PRIMARILY ABOUT ERICKSONIAN APPROACHES

Bandler, Richard, and Grinder, John. *Patterns of the hypnotic techniques of Milton H. Erickson, M.D. Volume I*. Cupertino, CA: Meta, 1975.

Bell-Gadsby, Cheryl, and Siegenberg, Anne. *Reclaiming herstory: Ericksonian solution-focused therapy for sexual abuse.* New York: Brunner/Mazel, 1996.

Combs, Gene, and Freedman, Jill. *Symbol, story and ceremony: Using metaphor in individual and family therapy.* New York: Norton, 1990.

Dolan, Yvonne. *A path with a heart: Ericksonian utilization with resistant and chronic patients.* New York: Brunner/Mazel, 1985.

Dolan, Yvonne. *Resolving sexual abuse: Solution-focused therapy and Ericksonian hypnosis for adult survivors.* New York: Norton, 1991.

Gilligan, Stephen. *Therapeutic trances: The cooperation principle in Ericksonian hypnotherapy.* New York: Brunner/Mazel, 1987.

Gordon, David, and Myers-Anderson, Maribeth. *Phoenix: therapeutic patterns of Milton H. Erickson.* Cupertino, CA: Meta, 1981.

Grinder, John, DeLozier, Judith, and Bandler, Richard. *Patterns of the hypnotic techniques of Milton H. Erickson, M.D. Volume 2.* Cupertino, CA: Meta, 1977.

Haley, Jay. *Uncommon therapy: The psychiatric techniques of Milton H. Erickson, M.D.* New York: Norton, 1973.

Haley, Jay. *Ordeal therapy: Unusual ways to change behavior.* San Francisco: Jossey-Bass, 1984.

Havens, Ronald, and Walters, Catherine. *Hypnotherapy scripts: A neo-Ericksonian approach to persuasive healing.* New York: Brunner/ Mazel, 1989.

Kershaw, Carol. *The couple's hypnotic dance: Creating Ericksonian strategies in marital therapy.* New York: Brunner/Mazel, 1992.

Klippstein, Hildegard. *Ericksonian hypnotherapeutic group inductions.* New York: Brunner/Mazel, 1991.

Lankton, Stephen (Editor). *Elements and dimensions of an Ericksonian approach.* New York: Brunner/Mazel, 1985. [Ericksonian Monographs #1]

Lankton, Stephen (Editor). *Central themes and principles of Ericksonian therapy.* New York: Brunner/Mazel, 1987. [Ericksonian Monographs #2]

Lankton, Stephen (Editor). *The broader implications of Ericksonian therapy.* New York: Brunner/Mazel, 1990. [Ericksonian Monographs #7]

Lankton, Stephen, Gilligan, Stephen, and Zeig, Jeffrey (Editors). *Views on Ericksonian brief bherapy, process and action.* New York: Brunner/Mazel, 1992. [Ericksonian Monographs #8]

Lankton, Stephen, and Lankton, Carol. *The answer within: A clinical framework of Ericksonian hypnotherapy.* New York: Brunner/Mazel, 1983.

Lankton, Stephen, and Lankton, Carol. *Enchantment and intervention in family therapy: Training in Ericksonian approaches.* New York: Brunner/Mazel, 1986.

Lankton, Stephen, and Lankton, Carol. *Tales of enchantment: Goal-oriented metaphors for adults and children in therapy.* New York: Brunner/Mazel, 1989.

Lankton, Stephen, and Zeig, Jeffrey (Editors). *Treatment of special populations with Ericksonian approaches.* New York: Brunner/Mazel, 1988. [Ericksonian Monographs #3]

Lankton, Stephen, and Zeig, Jeffrey (Editors). *Research, comparisons and medical applications of Ericksonian techniques.* New York: Brunner/Mazel, 1988. [Ericksonian Monographs #4]

Lankton, Stephen, and Zeig, Jeffrey (Editors). *Ericksonian hypnosis: Application, preparation, and research.* New York: Brunner/Mazel, 1989. [Ericksonian Monographs #5]

Lankton, Stephen, and Zeig, Jeffrey (Editors). *Extrapolations: Demonstrations of Ericksonian therapy.* New York: Brunner/Mazel, 1989. [Ericksonian Monographs #6]

Leva, Richard (Editor) *Psychotherapy; the listening voice: Rogers and Erickson.* Muncie, Indiana: Accelerated Development, 1988.

Lovern, John D. *Pathways to reality: Erickson-inspired treatment approaches to chemical dependency.* New York: Brunner/Mazel, 1991.

O'Hanlon, William Hudson. *Taproots: Underlying principles of Milton Erickson's therapy and hypnosis.* New York: Norton, 1987.

O'Hanlon, William H. and Martin, Michael. *Solution-oriented hypnosis: An Ericksonian approach.* New York: Norton, 1992.

Overholser, Lee C. *Ericksonian hypnosis: Handbook of clinical practice.* New York: Irvington, 1984.

Philips, Maggie, and Frederick, C. *Healing the divided self: Clinical and Ericksonian hypnotherapy for post-traumatic and dissociative conditions.* New York: Norton, 1995.

Ritterman, Michele. *Using hypnosis in family therapy.* San Francisco: Jossey-Bass, 1983.

Robles, Teresa. *A concert for four hemispheres in psychotherapy.* New York: Vantage Press, 1990.

Zeig, Jeffrey K. (Editor). *Ericksonian approaches to hypnosis and psychotherapy.* New York: Brunner/Mazel, 1982.

Zeig, Jeffrey K. (Editor). *Ericksonian psychotherapy. Volume I: Structures; Volume II: Clinical applications.* New York: Brunner/Mazel, 1985.

Zeig, Jeffrey K., and Stephen R. Lankton (Editors). *Developing Ericksonian therapy: State of the art.* New York: Brunner/ Mazel, 1988.